Gibraltar
HARDWARE

PRESENTS

DRUM HARDWARE SET-UP AND MAINTENANCE

BY ANDY DOERSCHUK

Choosing The Right Hardware

Performance And Maintenance Tips

Professional Set-ups

CREDITS PAGE

DRUM HARDWARE SET-UP AND MAINTENANCE

Author

Andy Doerschuk

Art Director

Kristine Ekstrand

Creative Director

John Roderick

Special Thanks

Brad Smith

Phil & Connie Hood

Paul Haggard

John Aldridge

Kaman Music Corporation is dedicating this book to the memory of Fred A. Hoey. Before working for Kaman Music Corporation, Fred was a prominent Southwestern performing percussionist. He was a charter member of the Percussive Arts Society and an educator, who influenced hundreds of percussionists throughout the United States.

Fred served as Sales Manager, Senior Percussion Product Advisor, and rose to Vice President of Sales for Kaman Music Corporation's C. Bruno & Son San Antonio division. During the early 1980s, Fred created the Gibraltar brand name and initiated Gibraltar's first designs. He was known at the Gibraltar factory as "Papa Gibraltar." His knowledge, leadership and friendship will be missed by all of us at Kaman Music Corporation and throughout the worldwide music community.

HAL•LEONARD™ CORPORATION

7777 W. BLUEMOUND RD. P.O. BOX 13819 MILWAUKEE, WI 53213

Contents

Introduction

I USED TO EDIT *DRUMS & DRUMMING* MAGAZINE. WE HAD A COLUMN CALLED "OFFBEAT," in which we featured a drumming story that was either humorous or weird — and hopefully both. Once we spoke to a Texas percussion retailer, Michael Henry, who listed all of the different malapropisms drummers had used when referring to their drum equipment. He told us about one guy who called his hi-hat pedal a "shoe-foot" and another who referred to his floor tom as "squatty legs." It's a funny story, but it contains a serious moral: If you want to be a drummer who is competing at any level, you should learn everything about drumming, including your musicianship, technique, sound, look and gear. In that sense, *Drum Hardware Set Up And Maintenance* should be a small, but important part of your ongoing study.

Of course, the idea of dedicating an entire book to the subject of drum and percussion hardware might seem like an ostentatious extravagance to most non-drummers. After all, the hardware's just the metal stuff that holds up the drums and cymbals, isn't it? Yes, just as surgical tools are the metal thingamajigs that doctors use to cut open their patients.

All sarcasm aside, drummers regard their hardware with as much reverence as doctors do their tools. It's just human nature. No matter what field a person chooses to pursue, he or she concentrates on improving the skills necessary to excel, and in the process, refines the tools that are available. Naturally, this process of refinement, handed down from generation to generation, creates new technologies that hardly even resemble their rough-hewn predecessors.

Such is the case with drum and percussion hardware. For example, in the early 1900s, a number of old-fashioned bass drum pedals were actually tied to the drummer's foot — no springs, no toe-stops — and required sheer strength to operate, since the drummer had to suspend his or her foot in the air most of the time. Imagine trying to sell a pedal like that today. It would be the laughing-stock of any contemporary drum shop, sitting beside modern pedals with their space-age adjustment knobs and chain drives. Yet today's pedals probably wouldn't be quite so advanced if those early inventors hadn't put their reputations on the line, and tried to do something that had never been done before.

In a similar way, this book attempts to do something new, by chronicling the current state of drum and percussion hardware. In the following pages, we'll take a look at every type of modern hardware available, from stands to pedals to rack systems, and break each one down into its most basic elements. We'll suggest a number of different ways to set up your hardware, so that you can learn to customize your kit to best suit your style of playing. We'll offer a variety of valuable hardware repair and maintenance tips, for both long-term and emergency solutions. And we'll talk with some of today's top drummers and percussionists about the creative applications of their hardware setups.

TYPES OF HARDWARE

I T'S PRACTICALLY IMPOSSIBLE TO DRAMATICALLY REDESIGN THE BASIC elements of percussion instruments. Just try to construct a square drum or a cymbal shaped like a roast turkey. Sure, you might be able to build both in your workshop, but neither would sound very good. For that reason, contemporary drum hardware has had to provide the same three essential functions since its inception: holding instruments in place, tensioning drums and pedaling. Over the years, though, modern drum companies have made such extensive use of new technologies, space-age materials, advanced manufacturing techniques and design innovations, that vintage percussion hardware now seems as outdated as the Model T. In this chapter we will look closely at the various types of hardware found in a modern drum and percussion setup.

Contemporary drum hardware has had to provide the same three essential functions since its inception: holding instruments in place, tensioning drums and pedaling.

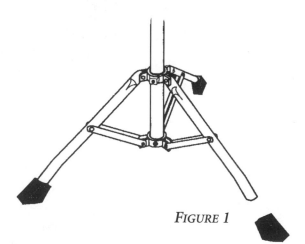

FIGURE 1

Instrument Holders

Hardware that holds instruments in a fixed position can be subdivided into three categories: stands, mounting hardware and rack systems.

Stands. A stand is a free-standing component, unattached to any other piece of hardware. On drum sets, stands are most-commonly used to hold cymbals and snare drums in place, although they are occasionally found supporting toms and hi-hats as well. Also, hand drums such as congas and timbales are almost always mounted on stands.

Most stands feature either a single- or double-braced tripod base. The term "brace" refers to the construction of the tripod legs. Single-braced tripods feature legs made of a solitary piece of stamped metal tipped with a

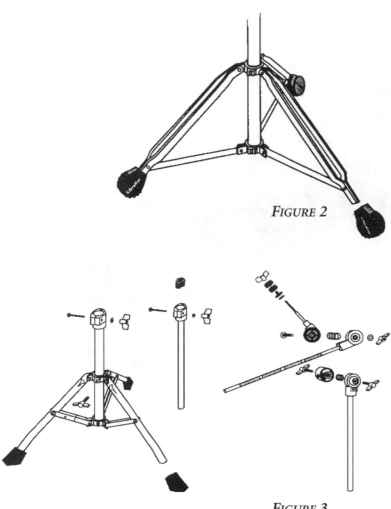

FIGURE 2

FIGURE 3

Most drummers feel that double-braced tripod stands are superior to single-braced stands, but in the harsh light of reality there are clear advantages to both styles.

rubber foot (Fig. 1). Double-braced tripod legs are made of two parallel pieces of stamped metal that meet and attach at both the rubber foot and the top collar (Fig. 2). The collar is the adjustment point that encircles and slides up and down the bottom shaft of the stand, allowing the tripod to be opened into a set-up position or folded-up for storage. The collar is held in position with a clamping mechanism, most commonly a wing-screw.

Many drummers feel that double-braced tripod stands are superior to single-braced stands, but in the harsh light of reality there are clear advantages to both styles. Double-braced stands offer increased durability and stability, as well as a chunkier, heavier look. Any drummer who plays his or her instrument hard and loud will benefit most from double-braced hardware. But if you happen to have a lighter touch, you might consider a single-braced setup. The rule of thumb is that single-braced hardware is less heavy (saving your back when you have to lug it around) and less costly (saving your bank account) than double-braced gear.

Just keep in mind that the issue of weight can be rendered a moot point by the type of material a stand is made of. For example, a double-braced aluminum stand will usually weigh less than a single-braced steel stand. But for the most part, aluminum hardware will prove to be more expensive than steel, and since aluminum is a light material it will provide slightly less stability and durability than steel, even on a double-braced stand. That explains why there has been a recent reemergence of a classic tripod-base design using elliptical legs (Fig. 3). These tubular tripod legs are made of cold-rolled steel tipped with rubber feet, and provide more stability than single-braced hardware with less weight than double-braced stands.

A further drum hardware tripod innovation was devised to allow hi-hat pedals, cymbal stands and tom stands to be easily set-up in situations where there is either limited space or unusual set-up requirements. The ATS (or advanced tripod system, Fig. 4) was invented by Randall May, who also is the creator of the May internal drum microphone mounting system. The primary difference between the ATS system and regular tripods is that one of its legs operates independently from the other two, providing a number of valuable applications that have been previously unavailable to drummers. For example, one leg can placed at a lower or higher level than the other two legs. This allows a drummer to position the stand close to the edge of drum risers and small stages by putting two legs at one level and the third at another, without sacrificing stability. The free-moving leg can also be adjusted to tilt the entire stand in any direction, or can simply be sent out further than the other two legs to support a particularly precarious load.

Most stands contain a system of elliptical telescoping shafts, or tiers. Each tier features a shaft of a slightly smaller diameter than the one into which it is inserted, allowing the stand to be raised to its fullest extension or packed away into a compact unit that is easy to transport. A clamping mechanism holds each shaft in place, the most basic being a wing-screw that tightens directly into the inner shaft. However, the most common clamping mechanism features a circular collar that is split vertically on one side and bolted or welded to the open end of a shaft (Fig. 5). Two metal lips extend from the collar on either side of the split, and a bolt is inserted horizontally through both lips. A wing-nut is then fitted onto the bolt, and as it is tightened it forces the two lips toward one another, applying pressure on the inner shaft.

By and large, better stands will feature a nylon bushing, split identically to the metal collar, that rests inside the collar. There are a number of advantages to using a nylon bushing. It eliminates metal-to-metal contact between one shaft and another, reducing the chances of unwanted rattles. It also provides a better gripping surface, because of nylon's natural "give." Plus, it's easier and cheaper to replace than the entire metal shaft when it wears out. Also, many stands are supplied with memory clamps (Fig. 6), which encircle the center shaft of the second and/or third tier of a stand, locking in place with a drum key. These adjustable clamps can be moved to any position on the stand's shaft, and enable a drummer to position that particular stand at the exact same height time after time, making for quicker and more efficient set-ups. In addition, memory clamps provide additional support, and are recommended for stands which are meant to endure harder and more sustained playing, such as snare stands, or support heavier instruments, such as conga stands.

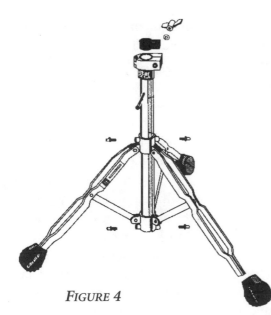

FIGURE 4

The primary difference between the ATS system and regular tripods is that one of its legs operates independently from the other two, providing a number of valuable applications.

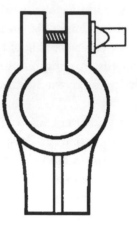

FIGURE 5   FIGURE 6

The number of tiers a stand features is largely dependent on its intended use. For example, a snare or conga stand will most likely have only two tiers. Since most drummers place their snare drums low between their legs, height is not an issue. Similarly, because congas are long, narrow drums, they can be mounted on a simple double-tiered stand and still be playable from a standing position. But since there are no standard positioning rules for cymbal setups, cymbal stands must offer a greater variety of height adjustments. For example, some drummers like to place their ride cymbal at elbow-height, while others prefer to play the ride over their heads, with their arm extended fully. Therefore, most cymbal stands feature a minimum of three tiers that allow the cymbal to be placed anywhere between 2-1/2 to 6 feet off the ground.

Cymbal stands come in two different configurations: straight stands and boom stands. Straight stands (Fig. 7) are very much self-descriptive: The upper-most tier extends vertically from the central shaft, and is topped by a cymbal-holding assembly. This assembly is most commonly composed of several elements: The cymbal ratchet is a circular, gear-toothed mechanism that is bolted onto an identically-machined gear-toothed piece fixed onto the tip of the cymbal stand's uppermost tier. High-end cymbal stands often feature a ball-and-socket tilter mechanism rather than a cymbal ratchet, which allows for more positioning flexibility. A metal pin with screw threads extends upward from the circular ratchet, onto which a washer is mounted. Normally, a nylon cymbal sleeve screws onto the pin, exposing 1/4" or so of the screw threads at the top of the pin. The cymbal sleeve rests on the metal washer and protects the cymbal from metal-to-metal contact with the pin. A felt washer is placed on the nylon sleeve to provide a cushioned surface on which the cymbal rests. The cymbal is then placed on the stand with the pin extending upward through the hole in the cymbal bell. Finally, a second felt washer is placed on the pin above the cymbal bell, and a wing-nut tightens down the entire assembly. By loosening the bolt that holds the cymbal ratchet to the upper tier, the angle of the cymbal can be adjusted to a number of positions.

Cymbal boom stands (Fig. 8) look very much like straight stands, except for their extra boom arm which extends horizontally outward from the top of the stand's shaft. The boom arm is commonly knurled, and positioned within a circular boom ratchet assembly, which looks and functions similar to the cymbal ratchet assembly. But rather than featuring a pin onto which a cymbal can be mounted, the boom ratchet has a central channel which corresponds in size to the boom arm. The boom ratchet has two wing-nuts on either side of it: one adjusts the angle of the boom arm and the other adjusts the length that the boom arm can be extended, as well as holding the arm securely in place. A typical cymbal ratchet is attached to the playing-end of the boom arm, and often, but not always, a counterweight will be attached to the far end of the boom arm to provide greater stability.

Whether you should use straight or boom stands for your cymbals will be determined mostly by the way you play and the size of your kit. If you use a small jazz kit with one mounted tom, you might only need two straight stands: one for a ride on the right-hand side, and the other for a crash on the left (for right-handed drummers. Vice-versa for lefties). But if you use more than one mounted tom, or a multiple cymbal setup featuring rides, crashes, splashes and Chinas, you will most likely have to use boom stands in order to position all of your cymbals within reach. Predictably, boom stands are heavier and more expensive than straight stands, so think carefully about your playing needs before planning your setup.

While cymbal stands are designed to allow the cymbal to move freely when struck, snare stands are made to hold the drum in a stationary

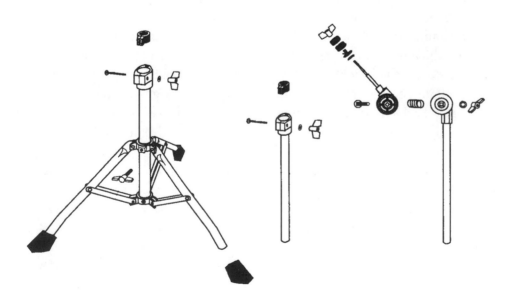

FIGURE 7

position. Most snare stands (Fig. 9) feature a typical tripod base, and a double-tiered shaft. At the top of the shaft is the snare basket, in which the snare drum sits. Most snare baskets feature three arms that extend outward from the stand's shaft with flanged "fingers" covered with rubber sleeves at the ends of the arms. At the base of the snare basket is a center handle nut tightening assembly, which forces the snare arms upward and inward simultaneously. Before placing the drum in the snare basket, the center handle nut should be loosened down so that the arms of the basket are almost fully opened. After the snare drum is in place, the center handle nut should be tightened up so that the basket's fingers lightly grip the snare drum. In most cases, the entire snare basket can be tilted using one of two methods: a ratchet that enables the snare to be tiled only forward and backward or a ball-and-socket system that allows the snare to be angled in any direction.

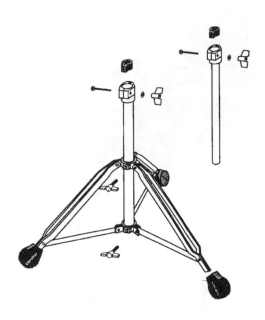

FIGURE 8

Although modern rack-mounting systems are threatening their very existence, floor tom legs and brackets remain a standard and vital part of most drum setups. Traditional floor toms feature three legs. Each leg is commonly bent in two places — outward, then downward — back toward the ground. This "elbow" is usually set up facing outward from the floor tom, which provides greater stability by creating a wider stance. The bottom of each leg is tipped with a rubber or plastic foot. The top of each floor tom leg is knurled, corresponding to the point where the leg is inserted into the bracket. Each bracket is secured to the floor tom with two to four screws, and grips the floor tom leg with a wingscrew-activated clamp or direct pressure from the wingscrew.

Most modern bongo stands feature a tripod base and two-tiered shaft (Fig. 10). The bongos are mounted on either a clamping system or an adjustable brace. The brace is attached to a standard tilter ratchet which allows the drums to be angled forward or backward. However, unlike bongos, which are normally played at an angle, congas are usually played with the heads perfectly horizontal to the ground. Therefore, conga stands don't require any sort of tilting system. Double conga stands (Fig. 11) feature an L-bracket mounting system which is attached directly to the top of the stand, a tripod base and two-tiered shaft. Two rubber-coated semi-circular conga shell supports clamp to the upper tier of the stand, to hold the congas straight and prevent the shells from touching metal.

Compared to most other stands, single conga stands (Fig. 12) have a rather unorthodox design. Instead of featuring a mounting system, single conga stands cradle the drum within either a circular or triangular three-legged frame. Rather than folding up like a standard tripod, the three legs telescope in and out for height adjustment, storage and transport, and are held in place with a clamping mechanism or a wing-screw. Three sets of rubber rollers attach to the circular frame to cradle the drum without marring its surface. Each set features two rollers, mounted vertically at either end of an arm which swings freely from a knurled metal rod. The rods are secured with wing-screws in holes bored horizontally through the top of the upper leg shafts. Locking casters are also a common feature on single conga stand legs, allowing the drum to either be easily moved or locked in place.

While all the previously discussed stands hold instruments in fixed positions, percussion tables (Fig. 13) simply provide a flat surface upon which any number of small hand-percussion instruments are placed. Percussion tables are usually supported by a standard tripod base or two T-leg assemblies with a double-tier shaft. A four-armed table-mounting plate is attached with a wing-bolt to the top of the stand, onto which the table top is screwed. Most commonly, the table top is covered with a soft felt surface to protect the instruments, and is bordered by a lip which extends upward beyond the surface of the table top to prevent instruments from falling to the ground.

Mounting Hardware. It can be argued convincingly that practically every previously-discussed stand contains some sort of mounting hardware, whether it be a cymbal mount or snare basket. However, mounting hardware, as it is commonly known, is more integrally involved with the instrument it supports. A traditional tom mount is probably the most familiar form of mounting hardware. Generally, a tom mount has two arms: one which is inserted into a metal bracket on the mounted tom and the other into a metal bracket on the bass drum. The tom mount

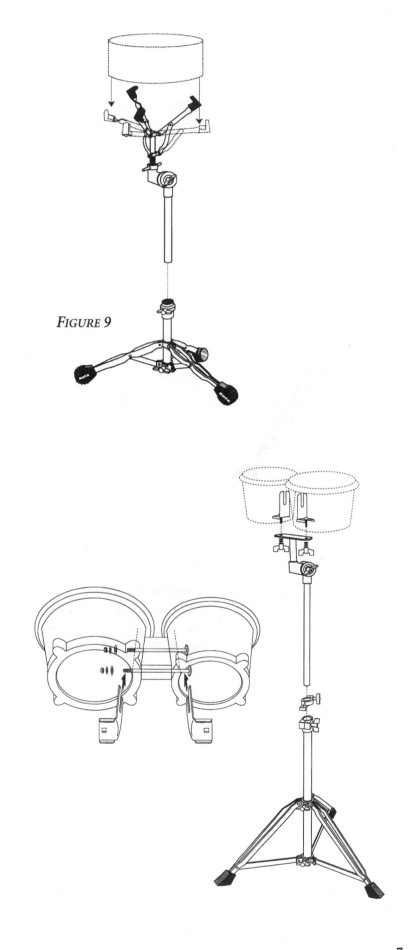

FIGURE 9

is held securely by wing screws in both brackets, and is commonly supplied with memory clamps on both arms for quick and accurate set-up.

Tom mounts come in a variety of styles. Perhaps the most traditional has an L-shape, with two hollow pipes joined by a ratchet, which allows the angle of the tom to be adjustable. Some drummers find this style of ratchet prohibitive in terms of tom placement, and prefer the more modern tom mount which features a ball-and-socket clamp, allowing the drum to be moved into a greater number of positions.

There is a growing contingent of drummers, however, who feel that these types of mounts are not only antiquated, but actually negatively affect the drum sound. Their argument is grounded in practical physics. Traditional tom mounts require either end of the tom arm to protrude through the shell of the bass drum and mounted tom, and receiver brackets in both drums that have to be hefty enough to support the mounted tom without damaging the shell. All this metal interrupts the free vibration of the shell, somewhat deadening both drums.

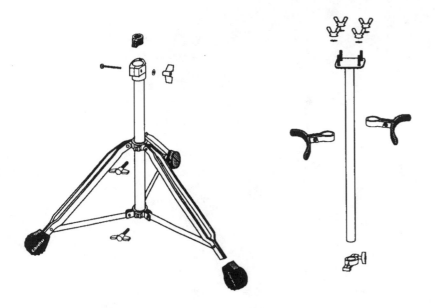

FIGURE 11

For that reason, several companies have developed tom mounting systems that eliminate the need to fasten additional hunks of metal to the shell. Pioneered by the RIMS system, these tom mounts usually employ a semi-circular bracket that attaches to a number of the mounted tom's tension rods. The upper drum hoop rests on the bracket, and the drum is held in place by its tension rods, so that there is no need to have a bracket attached to the drum or a tom arm protruding through the shell. Since drummers commonly desire less resonance in their bass drum than in their mounted tom, and consequently worry less about how freely their bass drum shell vibrates, this type of tom mount is often held by a traditional bass drum bracket. But still, there exists a segment of the drumming community that is fanatical about bass drum shell vibration. For them, tension-rod tom mounts can be attached to either free-standing stands or rack systems.

In addition to tom-toms, hand percussion instruments also require mounting systems. For many years, hand percussionists had to improvise mounting systems for their setups — using industrial clamps, cymbal stands, even clothespins — since most drum companies largely focused on drum-set hardware. Lately, though, greater attention has been paid to the equipment needs of hand-percussionists. Mounting systems for tambourines, cowbells, triangles, woodblocks and bongo drums are readily available. Each has its own unique clamping system which adapts not only to the instrument's profile, but to traditional support hardware, such as stands and rack systems. In addition to individual percussion mounts, manufacturers also offer percussion bars, which allow up to ten instruments to be mounted on knurled posts. These posts extend from a central arm which can be clamped to either a stand or rack system.

Rack Systems. Drum rack systems are like the skeleton of a drum or percussion setup, holding the various drums, cymbals and other percussion instruments securely in place. In recent years racks have become an accepted standard for a number of reasons, both practical and cosmetic. Combined with the use of tension-rod mounting systems, drum racks allow drummers to completely remove mounting hardware from their toms, bass drums and even floor toms. Because of the large number of modular parts options that are available, rack systems allow much more flexibility for complex positioning of drums and cymbals than standard drum set hardware can offer. Plus, rack systems — like double-bass drum setups — have become a fashion statement among certain segments of the drumming community, particularly with heavy metal drummers. Just turn on MTV and within minutes you are likely to see a drummer swinging from the upper tier of his rack with wild abandon.

Although the look of your kit is certainly an important consideration, for the purpose of this book, we will focus on the more pragmatic uses of rack systems. For the most part, the construction of rack systems is very simple. Most consist of round or square bars that serve as horizontal support bars as well as legs. These are held together by clamps — kind of like adult

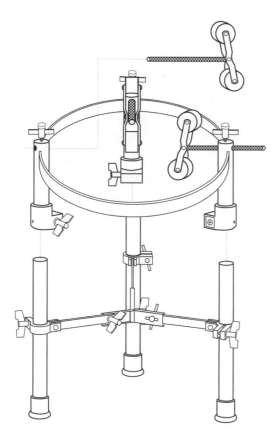

FIGURE 12

Tinker Toys. The bars are commonly hollow aluminum or steel tubing, available as straight or curved segments, and in a number of different lengths. This enables drummers to use rack systems for any type of kit, from the most conservative four-piece to a huge six-bass-drum, multiple tom and cymbal configuration.

There are several types of clamps used in most rack systems, and their most important duty is to grip firmly, without any slippage. Although all the clamps are essential, the basic multi-clamp is the key to the whole assemblage (Fig. 14). A multi-clamp features two clamping mechanisms that are tensioned with T-screws: one attaches to the support bar and another holds a drum mount or cymbal arm. Most often, the clamp that holds the multi-clamp to the rack encircles the circumference of the bar, and opens on a hinge when the t-screw is loosened, allowing for quick set-up and break-down. Because of its 360° contact with the rack's bar, a multi-clamp can achieve a variety of angles leaning toward or away from the drummer. On the other hand, the clamp that holds the mounting arm works more like a vice, pulling a thick, hinged metal plate into the clamp using two drum-key headed screws or wing screws. These screws extend through the metal plate and into the multi-clamp, straddling either side of a V-shaped indentation on the inner face of the metal plate. The length of the screws allows the metal plate to be extended far enough away from the multi-clamp to accept either a thick tom arm or a thinner cymbal arm, and the metal plate's hinge allows for easy set-up and tear-down. Most rack systems are supplied with standard memory clamps for accurate and quick positioning of multi-clamps.

Because of the large variety of possible uses of straight and curved support bars, there are two types of clamps which attach a rack's support bar to the legs. On a basic rack featuring a single straight bar across the front of the kit (Fig. 15), T-clamps are usually used to connect the legs to the support bar (Fig. 16). A T-clamp contains two circular clamping mechanisms that are large enough to accept the rack's tubing, and are activated with a T-screw. These clamping mechanisms are positioned at 90° angles, so that the leg clamp faces downward while the support bar's clamp faces horizontally. T-clamps are also effective in a slightly larger basic rack using straight side extension bars (Fig. 17). In this case two T-clamps are attached to each leg,

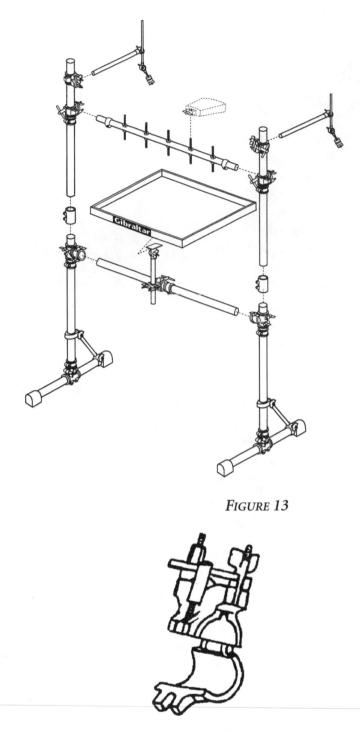

FIGURE 13

FIGURE 14

FIGURE 15

stacked one above the other. The support-bar clamping mechanism of the upper T-clamp faces across the front of the kit while the support-bar clamping mechanism of the lower T-clamp faces toward the back of the kit.

Besides the obvious difference in design between the stand-alone single-bar rack and a rack with side extension bars, the ability to stabilize each rack also takes on its own unique characteristics. A rack with side extensions is supported by legs at all four corners. However, a stand-alone rack only has two legs, and therefore requires a brace on each leg (Fig. 18). These braces extend backward and supply a third and fourth leg support.

For larger, more elaborate racks, drummers often want two horizontal support bars to join at an angle without the use of a leg. The adjustable angle clamp serves this purpose (Fig. 19), replacing the need to stack two T-clamps on a single leg. Adjustable angle clamps feature two clamping mechanisms joined by a wing-screw that permits the two clamps to be positioned at a variety of angles. This allows the rack to more easily and naturally wrap around the drummer with a large number of drums, cymbals and percussion instruments. Most commonly, when adjustable angle clamps are employed in a rack, the legs are clamped to the structure with right-angle clamps (Fig. 20) rather than T-clamps. Although both types of leg-supporting clamps feature clamping mechanisms that are at 90° angles, the right-angle clamp is a smaller and stronger alternative.

You might have guessed by now that as your setup becomes more elaborate, so does your rack. For the ultimate huge setup you should consider a two-tiered rack system (Fig. 21). These racks resemble cages, with standard support bars positioned across the front of the kit and side extensions, and an upper tier of bars running parallel to the lower tier. The legs of a two-tiered rack system are twice the length of standard rack legs, allowing T-clamps to be installed in the center of the leg for the lower support bars and at the top for the upper bars. The standard application is to mount all the tom toms on the lower tier and the cymbals on the upper tier.

Memory clamps are recommended for stands which are meant to endure harder and more sustained playing, such as snare stands, or support heavier instruments, such as conga stands.

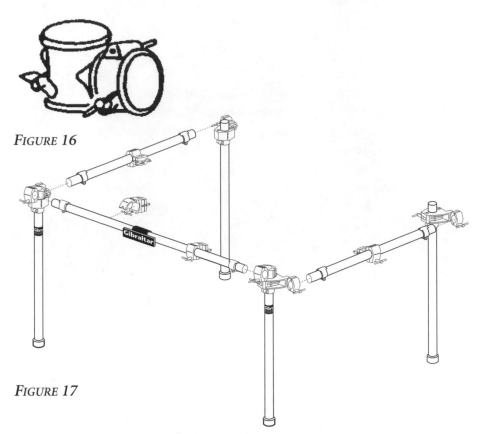

FIGURE 16

FIGURE 17

This makes for a striking drum-set profile, since the cymbal arms are actually mounted upside-down, suspending the cymbals from the top tier.

One of the interesting side-effects is that many aspects of drum rack technology can be integrated with traditional drum-set hardware. Many of today's rack clamps can be retrofitted to tom mounts, hi-hat stands and cymbal stands to hold extra cymbals, drums and percussion instruments in places where a traditional floor-stand wouldn't be able to squeeze. Now drummers who prefer using traditional cymbal stands can avoid mounting toms from a bass-drum mount by using a spanner system (Fig. 22). This positions a single horizontal rack-bar across the front of the drum kit, which attaches to cymbal stands on either side of the kit. In this type of setup, it is advisable to use heavy-duty double-braced cymbal stands to support the horizontal bar — otherwise you may experience an unacceptable degree of instability.

Tensioning Hardware

There is an obvious question that needs to be asked: What's all this hubbub about metal parts interrupting the vibration of the drum shell, when every drum has to have a number of metal lugs attached to the shell in order to accept the drum's tension rods? It's an astute point, and one that has been heavily researched over the years. A number of drum companies employ a technique called nodal lug mounting, where the drum lugs are placed at points in the shells where the vibrations from stick hits converge. However, other drum companies eschew this notion, and stick their lugs wherever they darn well feel like it. Amazingly, through, most drums can be tuned to sound just fine, no matter where the lugs are mounted on the shell. Needless to say, philosophies often clash in the drum manufacturing community, and it can be difficult at best to figure out who's right and who's wrong. Nevertheless, all drums require tensioning systems that are composed of three elements: counterhoops (or simply hoops or rims), lugs and tension rods.

Counterhoops. Hoops are commonly made of a circular piece of steel or brass that is slightly larger in diameter than the drum it is intended to be installed on. The most common type of hoop is made of a cold-rolled piece of steel that is bent and welded into a perfect circle. The other, more desirable style is a die-cast hoop, which is cast in a mold and therefore doesn't have any welds. A cold-rolled hoop features holes stamped into the metal through which the tension rods are inserted, while the die-cast hoop contains holes that are an integral result of the casting process. In either case, the holes should correspond exactly to the placement of the lugs around the outside of the drum shell. The outer edge of most contemporary hoops is flanged outward or inward, in order to allow drummers to perform rimshots without breaking an inordinate number of drum sticks on what would otherwise be a sharp edge. Bottom, snare-side snare drum hoops also have two horizontal slots in addition to the tension-rod holes, through which passes the cord or tape that attaches the snare drum strands to the throw-off.

Tension Rods & Lugs. In essence, tension rods are flat-nosed straight-sided screws that are inserted through the holes in the hoops and into the corresponding lugs. These days, most tension rods have a square head that corresponds to the universal drum key. Lugs commonly take on one of two forms: single- and long-lugs. Single lugs most commonly are small metal boxes, topped with a threaded tension-rod receptor. In contrast, long lugs span almost the entire width of the drum shell, and have tension-rod receptors at both ends. The tube lug is an old-style, low-mass long-lug design that has come back into fashion in recent years. It is a thin metal tube, most commonly made of brass, that is screwed to the shell at one or two points. By tightening the tension rods evenly into the lugs, the counterhoop is pulled toward the middle of the drum, which in turn applies tension to the drumhead.

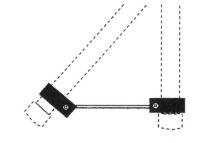

FIGURE 18

Unlike the other drums found in a drum set, the bass drum uses a slightly different system for drumhead tensioning. While bass drum lugs are commonly mounted on the shell in a similar fashion to snare drums and tom toms, bass drum counterhoops are usually made of a solid ring of wood or metal, without any tension rod holes. Instead, claw hooks grip the outer edge of the bass drum hoop. Bass drum tension rods have either T-handles or drum-key heads which protrude through holes in the center of the claw hooks, pulling the counterhoops inward when

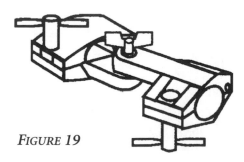

FIGURE 19

tightened.

Other Drumhead Tensioning Hardware. Designers have always experimented with tensioning hardware designs in an effort to relieve the shell of all intrusive metal parts. Some companies have tried rope-tensioning designs, in which nylon cords are strung between the two counterhoops. Another, more popular tensioning arrangement employs a process called a free-floating system, which is most often found in snare drum designs. In this process a drum shell is positioned between two counterhoops. Long tube-like lugs that don't touch the drum shell are held in position by the tightened tension rods.

Snare Throw-Offs And Butt Plates. Even though snare drum throw-offs (or strainers) aren't involved with the drumhead tensioning process, their purpose, nonetheless, is to provide tension on the snare strands. There are two throw-off designs that are accepted as industry standards. The most typical one features an arm that moves from side to side, parallel to the shell, while the other has an arm that pulls away from the shell and downward from the upper hoop. In both cases the snare strands are pulled taut when the arm is locked in a vertical position and are released when the arm is in a horizontal position. Either cord or tape is used to attach the snare strands to the bottom of the throw off, which moves up and down in unison with the throw-off arm. Most throw offs also have a knurled fine-tuning adjustment knob that allows you to loosen or tighten the snare strands. The snare butt is located directly opposite the throw-off, on the other side of the drum, and its purpose is to simply hold the snare strands firmly. It usually consists of a simple clamp that is tightened with two screws, although some snare butts also feature a fine-tuning knob to adjust the tension on the snare strands, just like the throw off. Both the throw off and the snare butt are normally affixed to the drum shell with two screws.

FIGURE 20

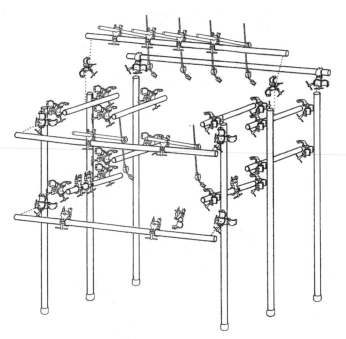

FIGURE 21

Pedals

Of all the various types of hardware that have been developed over the years, pedals have most expanded drummers' creative capabilities. Once limited by what they could physically play with their two hands, drummers could now integrate both feet, thereby doubling their capacity for expression. The traditional pedal setup consists of a bass drum pedal and a hi-hat, and although they are both activated similarly, their sound, design and function are radically different.

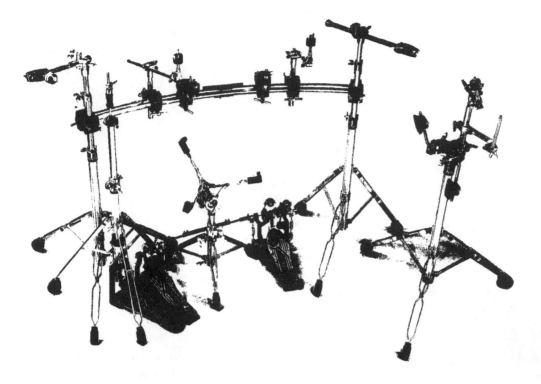

FIGURE 22

Pedals are similar to drum sticks. They are both tools used for coaxing sound from an instrument. After years of experimenting with various types, most drummers remain loyal to particular pedals that have exactly the right "feel" for their style of drumming and type of technique — just like sticks. But while the feel of a stick is determined by its length, shape and tip, a pedal's feel is produced by its machinery.

To a novice, it might seem logical that the best pedal will have the smoothest and fastest response. But while there are certainly a great many drummers who would desire those characteristics, there are also others who want a stiffer response. Surprisingly, these differences don't divide down any particular musical lines. For example, you are likely to find a quiet jazz drummer and a heavy-handed rocker who both prefer the exact same pedals. So the challenge is to experiment as much as possible. Spend some time in stores testing pedals. Look at the number of options they offer. Keep in mind that you don't need the pedal with the most bells and whistles if you won't end up using all of them. After all, as you add more moving parts to a pedal, you also increase the number of places where it can break or wear-out. Therefore, it's best to look for a user-friendly pedal that allows you to employ common tools such as a drum key, provides easily-accessible adjustment points and allows you to quickly replace broken or worn-out parts.

Single Bass Drum Pedals. The design of bass drum pedals has become increasingly complex in recent years, yet all pedals contain the same basic anatomy (Fig. 23). A cast pedal frame supplies the chassis on which all the various parts are dependent. The frame has a squared-off U-shape, with two arms rising straight upward from a metal base. At the top of each arm

After years of experimenting with various types, most drummers remain loyal to particular pedals that have exactly the right "feel" for their style of drumming and type of technique — just like sticks.

FIGURE 23

FIGURE 24

facing toward the center of the pedal is a swivel cam, most often riding on ball-bearings. A shaft spans the distance between the two arms, which is inserted into receptors in either swivel cam. A beater hub is held in the center of the shaft, usually by two screws. The bass drum beater is a metal shaft topped by a beater ball, and is inserted into a hole in the hub, which is held in place with a wing-screw. One end of either a bicycle-chain, metal strip or leather strap attaches to the beater hub, while the other end attaches to the top of the pedal board, passing through the center of the frame in the process. The pedal board consists of a foot plate and a heel plate, connected by a hinge. The heel plate sits flat on the floor, while the foot plate is angled up toward the top of the frame. A Y-shaped radius rod attaches to the underside of the footboard's heel plate with two screws. Both ends of the radius rod are flanged to create a tip which inserts into corresponding receptor holes at the base of the frame, holding the pedal board in place. A spring connects to the cam assembly and a receptor in the base of the frame, which pulls the pedal back from the head when the pedal board isn't depressed, and provides adjustable tension to the pedal board. A clamp on the drum-side of the pedal frame's base securely holds the pedal to the bass drum hoop using a wing screw. On most pedals, the bass drum hoop clamp features a wingscrew that is difficult to access while the pedal is attached to the drum. However, some innovative drum companies have redesigned this mechanism so that the thumb-screw extends beyond the top of the pedal frame, making attaching and detaching the pedal significantly easier. Finally, heavy-duty anchor screws with pointed tips are inserted on either side of the frame's base angled toward the bass drum. The tips of the anchor screws dig into the floor, inhibiting forward bass drum movement.

That's a basic pedal design, but there are plenty of options on the market. As mentioned earlier, pedals can be activated with either a bicycle chain, metal strip or leather strap, and there are convincing arguments for using any of them. Proponents of bicycle-chain drives point to the strength, power and accuracy that the chain provides. On the other hand, a number of drummers argue that the metal-on-metal contact of a bicycle chain drive is too noisy, and that a leather strap provides a more flexible action, with more "give," and is especially appropriate for quiet, subtle playing. Pedals that use a strip of metal provide perhaps the most direct action from the pedal board to the beater,

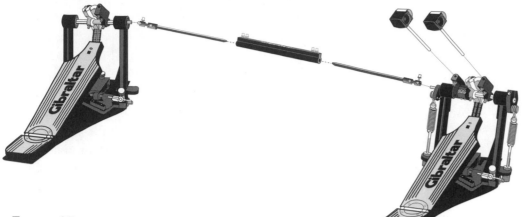

FIGURE 25

although they are generally not as strong as a chain-drive. An important factor to keep in mind when choosing your pedal is that among your three choices for pedal drives, the strap is the quickest and easiest to replace when broken, while most bicycle chains and metal strips are practically impossible to replace during an on-the-gig disaster. However, a recent development that has proved to be very useful can be found on new Gibraltar chain-drive pedals. On older-style pedals, the bicycle-chain linkage was riveted to the beater hub, but new Gibraltar pedals feature chains that are replaceable with a drum key.

Bass drum beaters also come in a variety of forms. The most traditional is the felt beater, which gives a solid, slightly muffled attack, and is available in both round and square styles. In general, a square felt beater is slightly louder, with greater attack than the round felt beater. In addition to felt, beaters are also available in wood and plastic — both of which produce a brighter, louder slap than their felt counterparts. Some companies provide dual-surface beaters with one side made of felt and the other made of either wood or plastic, that allow drummers to quickly and easily change their bass drum sound. In the last several years, a number of companies have experimented with the mass and shape of bass drum beaters, often reducing the size of the impact area or tapering the sides of the beater head. Another recently-popular beater option is the use of bass drum beater shaft counter weights, which screw onto the beater shaft. Moving the counter weight up and down the shaft fine-tunes the action of the pedal in tandem with the pedal spring adjustments. When choosing your beater, keep in mind that wood and plastic are more destructive to bass drumheads. If you want the high-end slap of wood or plastic you should consider using a beater pad. This pad affixes to the bass drumhead at the point of impact, and lengthens the life of the head, as well as adding slightly more "punch" to the bass drum sound.

Beater hubs also come in a variety of forms. For strap-drive pedals, beater hubs are most often simple boxes, with a tapered side where the strap rests on the hub. For chain-drive pedals, the beater hub can feature either an indented channel in which the bicycle chain rests, or a round sprocket with

Once limited by what they could physically play with their two hands, drummers could integrate both feet, thereby doubling their capacity for expression.

HARDWARE
CHAPTER 1

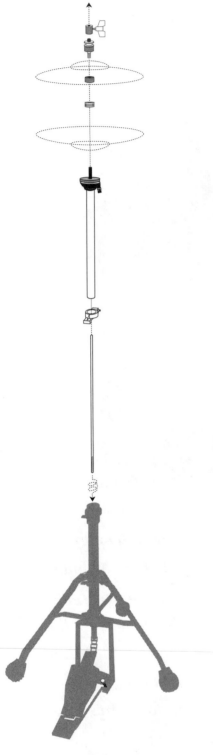

FIGURE 26

teeth that correspond to the holes in the chain — as well as pedals that combine both channels and sprockets. One of the ongoing troubles with traditional bass drum beater hubs is that if they were adjustable — in order to change the angle of the beater — they usually would also have an affect on the angle of the pedal board. However, in recent years, pedals have been introduced which offer an independently-adjustable beater hub (Fig. 24) and pedal board, which has proven to be a preferred alternative.

Another recent bass drum pedal option for which many drummers have opted is a footboard plate. This foot-shaped metal plate connects to the underside of the footboard's heel plate and to the bottom of the pedal's frame, replacing the standard radius rod. The footboard plate eliminates heel plate movement and helps to stabilize the entire pedal — although it also makes the pedal slightly more cumbersome to pack away and transport.

Hand percussionists have begun to incorporate a greater number of pedals into their setups. Although a few use them for bass drums, most attach them to cowbells for foot-activation. For this purpose, manufacturers have invented a cowbell bass-drum pedal mount that holds the cowbell vertically in line with the pedal's beater. The cowbell bass-pedal mount usually features an arm that is clamped into the pedal's bass-drum hoop clamp, and two rubber-tipped legs to inhibit unwanted forward movement.

Double-Bass Drum Pedals. Even though the concept for double-bass pedals has been around for a long time, their popularity really took off in the '70s, when rock drummers grew tired of lugging around two bass drums. Not only is there a great proliferation of double-pedals today, but they are also available in both right- and left-handed (or footed) models. In a typical double-pedal setup (Fig. 25), the primary pedal attaches to the bass drum hoop and the secondary pedal is positioned between the hi-hat pedal and the snare drum stand. Double pedals have many of the same characteristics as single pedals, with a couple significant differences.

The primary pedal works the same way as a single pedal, and in fact, most double pedals are designed to be modular, so that the primary pedal can be used alone as a single pedal. The main difference is that the primary pedal contains two separate spring assemblies, drive shafts, beater hubs and bass drum beaters on either side of the pedal frame. For right-handed drummers, the footboard of the secondary pedal activates the left beater assembly of the primary pedal through a shaft that connects the primary pedal's left spring cam with the secondary pedal's only spring cam, while the primary pedal activates the right beater assembly. The shaft connecting the two pedals usually consists of two or three separate lengths connected with U-joints, which allows the entire shaft to more easily wrap around snare drum and cymbal stands.

Even though primary pedals have two spring assemblies — one for each beater — the secondary pedal also features its own spring assembly, to adjust the feel of its pedal board. Also, since secondary pedals aren't attached to a bass drum, they most often come with footboard plates to provide greater stability. It is recommended to make use of any anchor screws on the secondary pedal, and to even retrofit an additional pedal anchor to the front of the secondary pedal to counteract unwanted forward movement.

Hi-Hat Pedals. Okay, some drummers call them pedals, others call them stands, but the truth is that hi-hat hardware consists of a pedal

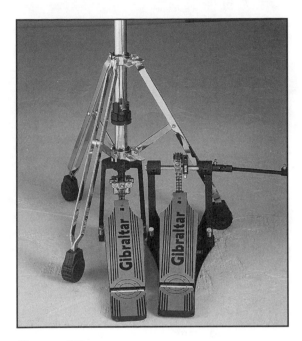

FIGURE 27

attached to a stand. Nevertheless, we're going to call them pedals, okay?

Basic hi-hat pedals (Fig. 26) feature a tripod base out of which rises a shaft, similar to a cymbal stand. A square metal frame is bolted to the bottom of the shaft, between the legs of the tripod. Like a bass drum pedal, the hi-hat footboard features a foot plate hinged to a heel plate, which is attached to the metal frame with a radius rod. The top of the foot plate is attached to the bottom pull rod. One or two inner or outer springs draw the pull rod upwards when the pedal is not being depressed. A wing screw holds the upper shaft in the stand's bottom shaft, which is topped by a hi-hat cup assembly. This assembly consists of a plastic or nylon cup with a hollow tube rising from its center. A metal washer is inserted around the tube, topped with a felt washer to protect the cymbal, which sits bell-down in the cup assembly. The bottom of the upper pull rod is threaded, and screws into a receptor at the top of the lower pull rod. The upper pull rod extends upward through the cup assembly's center tube, which is where the hi-hat clutch is attached. The clutch consists of a central metal tube, threaded on the outside, that is slightly larger than the upper pull rod. At the top of the tube, a wing screw holds the clutch firmly to the pull rod. Two felt washers hold the cymbal bell-up with the help of one or more round nuts that screw onto the threaded tube. The clutch clamps the top hi-hat cymbal to the pull rod, so that the cymbals clash together when the pedal board is depressed and are pulled apart when the foot pressure is released.

Hi-hat pedals normally don't offer as many adjustment possibilities as bass drum pedals, altough there are a few that can alter the hi-hat's feel. For example, some hi-hats feature a spring-tension adjustment that control the resistance of the pedal board, and some newer hi-hats include a pedal height adjustment, similar to certain bass pedals. Most hi-hats also feature a wingscrew that protrudes through the cup assembly, which alters the angle of the bottom hi-hat cymbal when it is activated. And now that the ATS tripod system is available on hi-hat pedals — allowing drummers to angle their hi-hats inward (Fig. 27) — the ATS system has proved to be as

You don't need the pedal with the most bells and whistles if you won't end up using all of them. As you add more moving parts to a pedal, you also increase the number of places where it can break or wear-out.

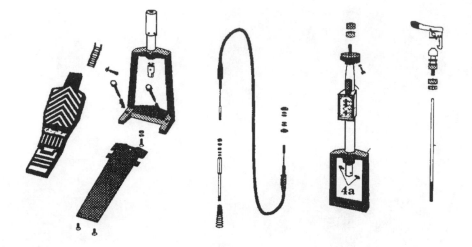

FIGURE 28

important to stands as RIMS was to tom mounting.

Cable Hi-Hats. Just a few years ago, it began to occur to drummers that there should be more than one place to position your hi-hat pedal, and that's how the cable hi-hat was born. Cable hi-hat systems (Fig. 28) combine a standard foot pedal, clutch, upper shaft and pull rod with a flexible tube through which a cable can move up or down. The cable attaches to a spring mechanism on the pedal's frame and another spring mechanism at the base of the upper shaft. When the pedal is depressed the cable pulls the top cymbal down, and springs push the top cymbal back up when the pedal is released. The upper shaft of the cable hi-hat can be attached to either a drum rack or stand using an extension arm.

However, cable hi-hats should come with a word of warning. Although they became the rage during the '80s, time has shown these systems to be far from infallible. To date, no one has introduced a cable hi-hat in which the cable doesn't regularly break without warning. As a result, a number of drum companies have either discontinued or severely scaled-back their cable hi-hat offerings. In other words, it's a great idea to use a cable hi-hat as a secondary pedal, but it isn't reliable enough to use as a primary pedal. So don't run out and replace your standard hi-hat pedal with a cable system.

Fixed Hi-Hat Mounts. These type of extension hi-hats were introduced for drummers don't require a foot-activated secondary hi-hat. Fixed hi-hat mounts, or X-hats, feature a standard hi-hat cup assmembly which is attached to a cymbal arm with an adjustable bracket, allowing the angle of the cymbals to be altered. However, rather than having a movable pull rod like a standard hi-hat pedal would, a stationary rod extends upward from the center of the cup assembly, onto which a hi-hat clutch is fitted. Higher-quality fixed hi-hat mounts feature a bottom cymbal tension adjustment that allows the user to make quick changes without having to fiddle around with the clutch, as well as a multi-clamp that enables the user to attach the hi-hats to cymbal stands or rack systems.

Other Pedal-Related Hardware. The addition of multiple pedals into drum setups made it difficult to find space for regular stands. As a result, new breeds of stands had to be invented to maximize the amount of available floor space. Many hi-hat pedals now feature tripod bases that swivel

Proponents of bicycle-chain drives point to the strength, power and accuracy that the chain provides. On the other hand, a number of drummers argue that the metal-on-metal contact of a bicycle chain drive is too noisy, and that a leather strap provides a more flexible action, with more "give," and is especially appropriate for quiet, subtle playing.

from side to side, making it much easier to tuck a secondary double bass pedal next to the hi-hat pedal. The single-leg snare stand was also invented to help open-up tight pedal setups. This stand has a standard snare basket and upper shaft, which fits into a single leg that is attached to a flat, round base assembly. An extension arm provides secondary support for the stand's central shaft from either a double-tom stand or a rack.

The drop clutch is another hardware innovation that sprang from the use of cable hi-hats. Since many drummers wanted to use a cable hi-hat as a secondary pedal in tandem with a regular hi-hat, the drop clutch allows a drummer to close the secondary hi-hat. By hitting the clutch's release arm with a stick, the wing screw's tension is disengaged, allowing the cymbal to be played in a closed position without holding down the pedal with your foot. Another device called a hi-hat stabilizer was invented to secure cable hi-hat pedals to other pieces of hardware, in order to prevent unwanted movement.

Drum Thrones

There is one piece of drum hardware that doesn't support or tune an instrument, which is often disregarded until it's too late, yet is vital to every drummer — the ostentatiously-named drum throne (Fig. 29). Any drummer who has had a throne disintegrate underneath him or her understands how embarrassing it can be. Therefore, if you can only afford to buy one double-braced piece of hardware, make sure it is your throne. Most thrones feature a heavy-duty tripod base, out of which rises two short tiers. The top tier attaches to a bracket screwed into the bottom of the seat, which is held in place with a wingscrew.

The method with which you adjust the height of the throne is essential in determining its strength. Less-expensive thrones feature a simple wingscrew that protrudes through the bottom tier, and bites into a series of

FIGURE 29

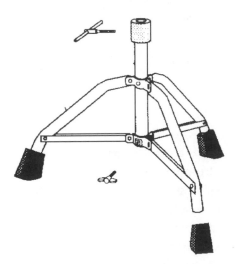
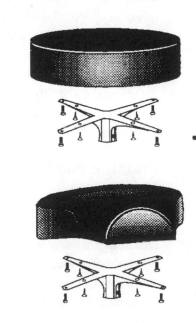

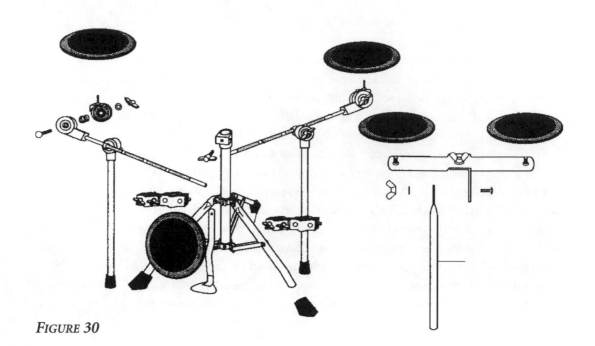

FIGURE 30

corresponding depressions in the top tier. Because of the incredible amount of stress that a throne must endure, this style is the least effective, since the wingscrew has to withstand the full pressure on its own. Much more effective, and more expensive, are stands that feature either a hydraulic system or a system where the top tier has large screw threads that correspond to screw threads in the lower tier.

In addition, drum thrones can also feature a variety of seat styles and sizes. The most common seat shapes are either circular or bicycle-seat shaped, and can be covered in any variety of cloth or synthetic materials. Most seats feature a foam cushion, although air-filled cushions have also become available in recent years. Whichever you choose, it's important to select the seat that will work best for your style and body. The seat should be large enough to adequately hold your weight, and yet not so large that it will inhibit the movement of your legs. It's also very important to select a throne that features a firm seat. Think of it as you would your car seat — you're going to spend a lot of time sitting on it, so it better offer you an adequate degree of support. Plus, the firmer it is, the longer it will last. Finally, when shopping for a throne, be sure to know exactly the height that you want to sit — you don't want to be stuck with a throne that is too high or low. As mentioned earlier, the ATS system is the newest drum throne innovation, allowing drummers for the first time the ability to lean the throne either toward or away from the set.

Practice Pad Kits

Although it can be argued that practice pads are not instruments, they are none-the-less used extensively by many drummers as substitutes for the real thing. As such, it is just as important to choose a practice pad setup that is suitable for your playing style. Most practice pad sets (Fig. 30) feature some sort of frame on which the various pads are mounted. Practice pad sets have traditionally included flimsy hardware, which was designed more for easy storage than stability. However, in recent years, manufacturers have constructed practice pad kits from modular rack system hardware, vastly increasing stability without forfeiting portability.

CHAPTER 2

BASIC SETUPS

UNLIKE GUITARISTS, KEYBOARDISTS, TRUMPETERS OR EVEN XYLOPHONE PLAYERS, today's drummers and percussionists enjoy the option of choosing a large number of instruments from a variety of potential sizes and sounds, and arranging them in any configuration that comes to mind. For that reason, no two drum sets — like no two drummers — are alike. Sure, there are plenty of four-piece kits out there, but take a closer look. One might have a 13" mounted tom, while another has a 12". Some drummers set their cymbals flat while others angle them. Some drummers sit high, others low . . . and on and on.

Most drummers love designing their dream kits. Just keep in mind when buying your first kit that most drum sets come only with mounting hardware for toms, basic tensioning hardware, and legs for floor toms and bass drums. This means that you have to buy your cymbals, pedals and stands separately, so be sure to work it into your budget. Most drum companies offer brand-specific hardware packages that simplify the decision-making process. However, there is a vast selection of hardware for today's drummers. Sit down and think about your set-up. How many stands do you need? Will they all be single- or double-braced? Do you have enough drums to justify buying a rack system, or do you want to play a little jazz kit? Do you want to sit high or low?

When you walk into your local drum shop you will see stacks of four and five drums from a variety of drum companies. These are perhaps the most common drum set-ups, and are called four- and five-piece kits, no matter how many cymbals, accessories or percussion instruments you add to them. Of course, the size of your kit is restricted by only your imagination and pocketbook, but there are certain sizes and configurations that have become

4 PIECE DRUM SET-UP
with basic hardware

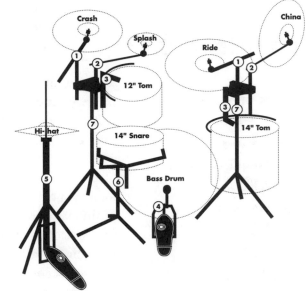

NOTE:
This set-up features medium and light weight/low mass stands to reduce weight.

PARTS GLOSSARY

MOUNTING SYSTEMS

(1) **SC-SBS**
SUPER BOOM (small)

(2) **SC-4425B-1**
CYMBAL BOOM ARM

(3) **SC-700HA**
PEARL™ STYLE TOM ARM (7/8" dia.)
with SC-670TB tom tom mounts and
R.I.M.S.™ tom mounting system

PEDALS

(4) **GASP**
AVENGER SERIES SINGLE PEDAL

(5) **JZ07**
JZ SERIES HI-HAT STAND

STANDS

(6) **JZ06**
JZ SERIES SNARE STAND

(7) **7513**
7500 SERIES PLATFORM STAND

5 PIECE DRUM SET-UP
with small rack and basic hardware

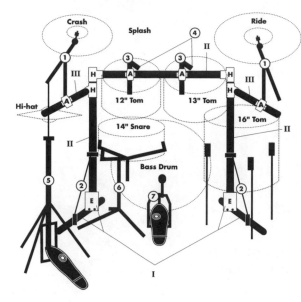

NOTE:
This set-up features a quick set up rack with minimal stands to reduce the overall size and weight.

PARTS GLOSSARY

CLAMPING DEVICES

A   **SC-GRSMC**
ROAD SERIES MULTI-CLAMP

B   **SC-GRSTL**
ROAD SERIES T-LEG CLAMP (part of I)

C   **SC-GPRTC**
POWER RACK T-CLAMP

MOUNTING SYSTEMS

①   **SC-SBS**
SUPER BOOM (small)

②   **SC-GPRLB**
POWER RACK LEG BRACE

③   **SC-700HA**
PEARL™ STYLE TOM ARM (7/8" dia.)

④   **SC-670TB**
PEARL™ STYLE TOM TOM MOUNTS
(not shown)

RACK TUBES

I   **SC-GRSTLA**
ROAD SERIES T-LEG ASSEMBLY

II   **SC-GPR36**
36" BAR

III   **SC-GPR24**
24" BAR

STANDS & PEDALS

⑤   **JZ07**
JZ SERIES HI-HAT STAND

⑥   **JZ06**
JZ SERIES SNARE STAND

⑦   **GASP**
AVENGER SERIES SINGLE PEDAL

standards in the drum manufacturing community.

Basic Drum Set Positioning. From the perspective of a right-handed drummer, most drum sets are assembled so that the bass pedal is played with the right foot. The smallest tom is mounted on top of the bass drum, directly in front of the drummer. The rest of the toms are positioned from high-to-low in an arch that wraps around the right side of the drummer, with the lowest floor tom off to the far right. The snare drum rests between the drummer's legs, usually directly in-line with the smallest tom. The hi-hat pedal is played with the left foot, and sits to the left of the snare drum. Crash cymbals are typically placed above and between the hi-hat and high tom, and above the floor tom. And the ride cymbal sits above and to the right-side of the bass drum.

Four-Piece Set. Four-piece kits most commonly feature a 20" to 24" bass drum, a 14" snare drum, a 12" or 13" tom mounted on an L-arm off of the bass drum and a 16" floor tom. In addition, a basic four-piece kit would include hi-hat cymbals, one or two crash cymbals and a ride cymbal. The additional hardware required for this kind of set-up would include a hi-hat pedal, a bass pedal, a snare stand, and two or three straight or boom cymbal stands. Hardware options include a double-bass pedal, remote hi-hat stand or cowbell/percussion mount.

Five-Piece Set. Five-piece sets are usually the same as four-piece sets with an extra 8" to 18" tom tacked on. One style has a T-shaped mounted tom arm coming out of the bass drum, which suspends toms from both arms. The hardware set-ups and options are very similar to the four-piece kit, except for one thing: You might find that you have a greater need for boom cymbal stands using this type of five-piece kit, since the ride is traditionally positioned right where the additional tom is mounted (on the right side of your bass drum). Another five-piece kit that has made something of a resurgence recently features a single mounted tom and two floor toms, and requires only a single L-arm tom mount.

Double-Bass Set. Thanks to drummers like Louie Bellson and Ginger Baker, double-bass drum setups are now well-established. The basic double-bass kits are five-, six- or seven-piece setups, depending on the number of floor toms and mounted toms they include. A typical six-piece double-bass kit has an 8" to 12" tom mounted on a single L-arm on one bass drum and a 10" to 14" tom on the other. A seven-piece double-bass kit has two toms mounted on a T-arm on one bass drum and a third tom on a single L-arm on the other bass drum. Generally, most double-bass kits require double-braced boom stands for all of your cymbals except for your hi-hat, since the cymbals have to be suspended high above the two bulky bass drums and multiple toms. Double-bass setup options are very similar to the basic four-piece kit, although it often seems as if double-bass drummers eventually buy a gong stand, for some mysterious reason.

When Racks Become A Necessity. As you add more drums and cymbals to your setup, you also must add just as many more stands to hold them. If you begin to get a little excessive you will literally run out of floor space before you run out of air space using traditional hardware. A large double-bass set with multiple toms and conventional stands becomes a Rube Goldberg nightmare of tangled tripod legs and boom arms that obscure both the drummer and the drum kit.

If you want to play a large kit, you should seriously consider using a rack system to mount most of your drums and cymbals. It becomes infinitely easier to position your instruments exactly where you want them using a rack system. Plus it makes your setup look much cleaner, and more high-tech.

But racks also offer plenty of acoustic benefits as well. They remove tom-mounting hardware from the bass drum shell, and by using a rack that wraps around the right side of the kit (from the player's perspective) you can mount the drums formerly known as "floor" toms on suspension mounts from the rack. This eliminates the need to attach floor tom legs and brackets to the drums, which makes a remarkable difference in the tone, clarity and volume. In addition, rack-mounting floor toms allow you to experiment more with their dimensions. These days more drummers are opting for "short" rather than "square" floor toms on their racks, and many of them insist that the difference in sound is dramatic.

When using a double-bass drum kit with remote hi-hat pedals, the space

6 PIECE DRUM SET-UP
with minimal tripod stands

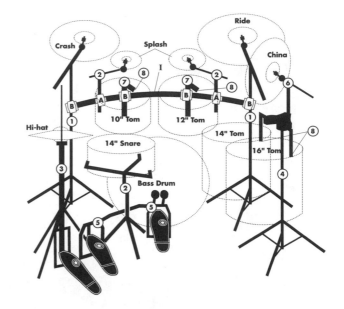

NOTE:
To reduce the amount of tripod stands used and improve positioning, this set-up utilizes Road Series rack accessories attached to the ATS Series tripod stands.

Keep in mind when buying your first kit that most drum sets come only with mounting hardware for toms, basic tensioning hardware, and legs for floor toms and bass drums.

PARTS GLOSSARY

CLAMPING DEVICES

A SC-GRSMC
ROAD SERIES MULTI-CLAMP

B SC-GRSSMC
ROAD SERIES SUPER MULTI-CLAMP

STANDS & PEDALS

(1) **ATS-095**
SHORT CYMBAL BOOM W/ ADVANCED TRIPOD SYSTEM

(2) **9506**
9500 SERIES SNARE STAND

(3) **ATS-07ML**
MOVABLE LEG HI-HAT W/ ADVANCED TRIPOD SYSTEM

(4) **ATS-13**
L-ROD STYLE DOUBLE TOM STAND W/ ADVANCED TRIPOD SYS.

(5) **GIDP-C**
INTRUDER SERIES DOUBLE PEDAL W/ CAM DRIVE

MOUNTING SYSTEMS

(6) **SC-4425B-1**
CYMBAL BOOM ARM

(7) **SC-LRM**
MEDIUM L-ROD (10.5 mm)

(8) **SC-STL2**
SUPER L-ROD TOM MOUNTS (not shown)

RACK TUBES

I SC-GPRSSS
SUPER SPANNER SYSTEM (46" curved bar with clamps)

between your snare stand, bass and hi-hat pedals will suddenly be very snug, possibly even making you set-up your pedals in an awkward fashion. The answer is to get a single-legged snare stand that is secured to the rack. And if there still isn't enough room to maneuver your feet, you might consider adding a legless rack-mounted hi-hat stand. In addition, your drum-set microphones can be mounted on your rack, which creates a super-clean setup without any obtrusive stands at all.

7 PIECE DRUM SET-UP

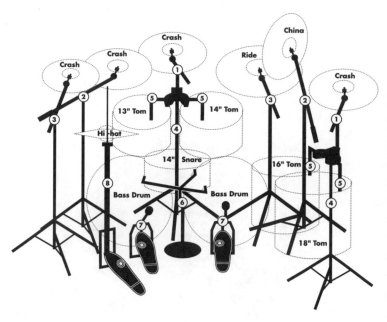

NOTE:
This set-up uses the Advanced Tripod System which maximizes each stands' center of gravity allowing a more stable mounting for larger drums and cymbals.

PARTS GLOSSARY

STANDS & MOUNTING SYSTEMS

① SC-SBS
SUPER BOOM (small)

② ATS-09L
LONG BOOM W/ ADVANCED TRIPOD SYSTEM

③ ATS-09M
MEDIUM BOOM W/ ADVANCED TRIPOD SYSTEM

④ ATS-13
DOUBLE L-ROD TOM STAND W/ ADVANCED TRIPOD SYSTEM

⑤ SC-STL2
SUPER L-ROD TOM MOUNT

⑥ 9506SL
SINGLE LEG SNARE STAND
(attached to ATS-13 double tom stand)

PEDALS

⑦ 9507NL
9500 SERIES NO LEG HI-HAT

⑧ GISP
INTRUDER SERIES SINGLE PEDAL

However, one doesn't need to play a huge drum set to find a rack system desirable. Some drummers use a single bar rack across the front of their kit in order to place their mounted toms on the rack rather than on the bass drum. And there are drummers who use a front bar with a side extension for a four-piece kit in order to mount their floor toms on suspension mounting systems rather than floor tom legs.

Basic Hand Percussion Rack Positioning. In addition, hand percussionists have eagerly adopted rack systems to organize their battery of drums, shakers and noisemakers. Most commonly, congas and timbales remain mounted on traditional stands with one-, two- or three-sided rack extensions surrounding the percussionist. These usually feature two tiers loaded with various instruments that are suspended within close reach of the player. Some are solidly-mounted, while others are suspended from cords, and still others are perched on a peg waiting to be grabbed and shaken. Somewhere within this cage, percussionists usually integrate a

When using a double-bass drum kit with remote hi-hat pedals, the space between your snare stand, bass and hi-hat pedals will suddenly be very snug, possibly even making you set-up your pedals in an awkward fashion.

table — which can be either rack-mounted or on legs — to hold the smaller instruments and toys.

Your choice of hardware can have a dramatic effect on your sound and image, and is as much of a statement of your individuality as the size and the color of your drums. So look closely at your style of drumming, your creative needs and your budget before you purchase a set of hardware.

CHAPTER 3

ARTISTS & THEIR SETUPS

T HE MANNER IN WHICH A PARTICULAR DRUM KIT IS SET UP CAN TELL YOU much about the style and technique of the drummer who plays it. For example, it's easy to guess the difference between a drummer who uses a huge double-bass cage setup and another who plays a four-piece kit with traditional straight cymbal stands. Even though most drummers and percussionists use stock hardware parts to assemble their setups, each kit is slightly, and sometimes radically, different from all the others.

Of course, the profile of your kit is at least partly determined by the length of your arms and legs, but much of it comes from the creative statement you want to make. Drum and percussion setups can look either complex or simple, high-tech or traditional, low-key or in-your-face. They can incorporate many or a few sounds or can be set up high or low. In fact, there are so many variables that most drummers spend years figuring out exactly the right angles and levels at which to place their various instruments.

Even the most accomplished drummer can feel surprisingly alienated when he or she sits down behind someone else's kit. The reason is simple. The angle of your toms, the height of your cymbals and the tension of your pedals help to define the type of drummer you are. So you need to feel comfortable and confident behind your drums if you want to successfully express yourself. If you have to struggle to make your way around the kit, you might want to rethink your setup.

The following artists might give you some new ideas. They are a cross section of the most successful and respected drummers and percussionists in the music business. Part of the reason they prospered in this competitive industry is that they have maximized the creative applications of their equipment. Using the same basic building blocks, they have each assembled their own personalized statements, for their own reasons.

> *Even the most accomplished drummer can feel surprisingly alienated when he or she sits down behind someone else's kit.*

MICHAEL BAKER CUT HIS TEETH drumming with Weather Report keyboardist Joe Zawinul, Police guitarist Andy Summers — with whom he used his first custom rack, a Yamaha prototype — and more recently with Whitney Houston. Baker had been using a Gibraltar rack with curved bars when he first started touring with Houston, but decided to put together a more unusual design for a gala television special that they were scheduled to record for HBO.

"I like racks, but I don't like to feel like I'm in a cage," he explains. "I wanted my cymbals to be suspended in the air, which I've seen a lot of drummers do, but I wanted it to be just a little bit different. So my drum tech and I designed this rack with two curved bars coming up over the kit from the back. They almost look like elephant tusks pointing outward toward the audience. All of my cymbals are hanging down from them, and nothing is connected in front, so you can't see how it's being held up, except from the back. I'm really happy with it, because it's unique. I've never seen anything quite like it.

"I was talking to Whitney's sound man," he continues, "and he really dug the rack, because it totally eliminates mike stands for the cymbals and hi-hats. We're using Shure mike clamps on the drums." Baker almost seems surprised to report that he has also noticed acoustic advantages to using his

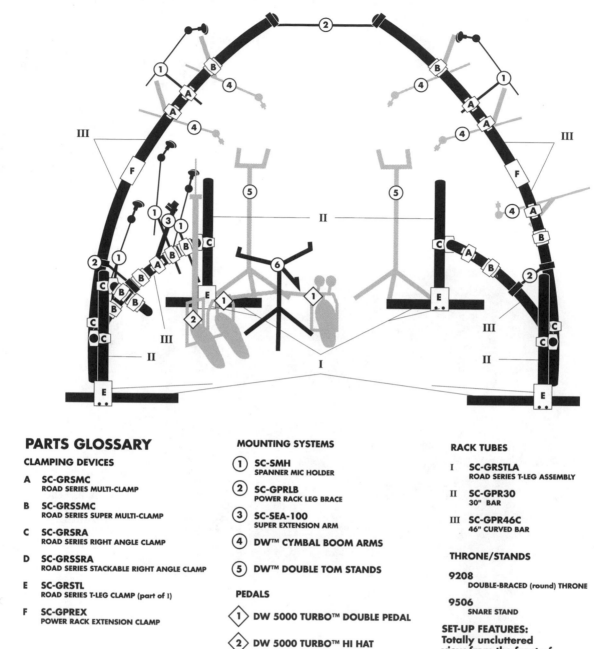

PARTS GLOSSARY

CLAMPING DEVICES

A **SC-GRSMC**
ROAD SERIES MULTI-CLAMP

B **SC-GRSSMC**
ROAD SERIES SUPER MULTI-CLAMP

C **SC-GRSRA**
ROAD SERIES RIGHT ANGLE CLAMP

D **SC-GRSSRA**
ROAD SERIES STACKABLE RIGHT ANGLE CLAMP

E **SC-GRSTL**
ROAD SERIES T-LEG CLAMP (part of I)

F **SC-GPREX**
POWER RACK EXTENSION CLAMP

MOUNTING SYSTEMS

① **SC-SMH**
SPANNER MIC HOLDER

② **SC-GPRLB**
POWER RACK LEG BRACE

③ **SC-SEA-100**
SUPER EXTENSION ARM

④ **DW™ CYMBAL BOOM ARMS**

⑤ **DW™ DOUBLE TOM STANDS**

PEDALS

◇1 **DW 5000 TURBO™ DOUBLE PEDAL**

◇2 **DW 5000 TURBO™ HI HAT**

RACK TUBES

I **SC-GRSTLA**
ROAD SERIES T-LEG ASSEMBLY

II **SC-GPR30**
30" BAR

III **SC-GPR46C**
46" CURVED BAR

THRONE/STANDS

9208
DOUBLE-BRACED (round) THRONE

9506
SNARE STAND

SET-UP FEATURES:
Totally uncluttered
view from the front of
the drumset. All mics,
floor toms and
cymbals are mounted
from the rack. From
the front, the
appearance suggests
that no drum rack is
being used.

rack: "The sound guy really dug the way the cymbals sounded because of the way they were suspended. Hanging like that, they seem to resonate more."

LUIS CONTE IS ONE OF THE BUSIEST HAND
percussionists in Los Angeles, performing
on soundtracks, albums and high-profile
tours. He was still using conventional drum-set
hardware and a table-stand when he began
touring with Madonna in 1987. "I used regular
stands for whatever I had to suspend off of the
floor, like timbales and bongos," Conte says. "It worked
for a while, but whenever the tech would set things up, I would have to go
tweak everything. Then I started to use a Gibraltar rack, and the placement of my setup stayed the same each time, and everything fit into it."

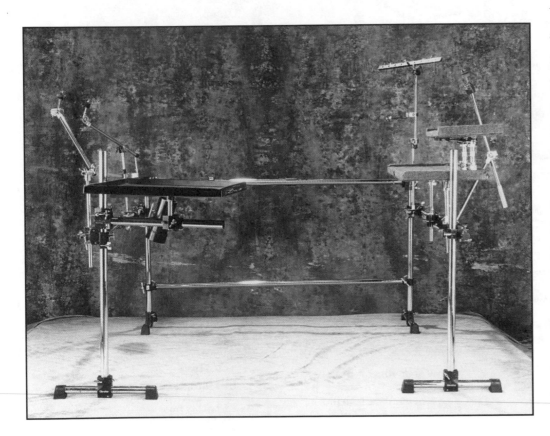

Conte says that he referred to the two-tiered rack that he used on the road with Madonna as "the condominium," and says that one of its best features was how easy it was to alter. "It's like Legos," he says, laughing. "I did the Steve Winwood tour after I came off the road with Madonna,

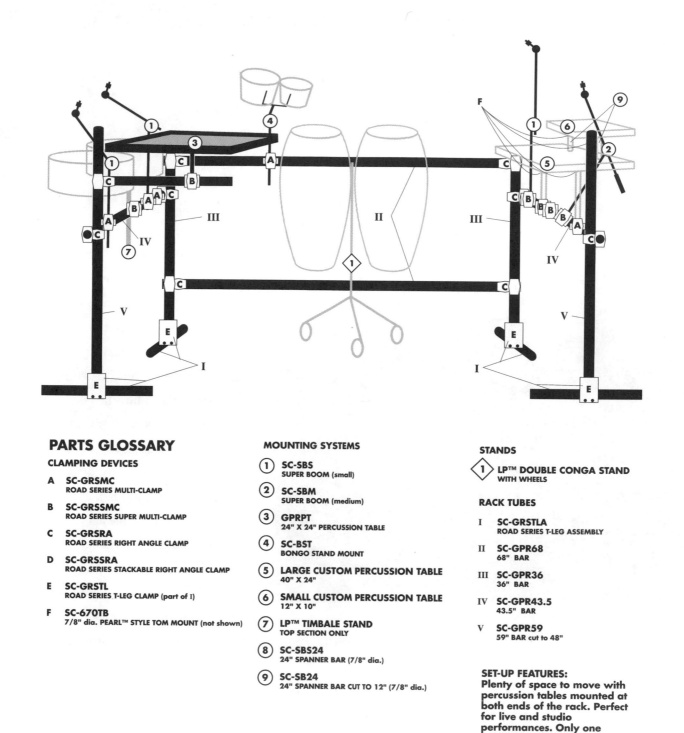

PARTS GLOSSARY

CLAMPING DEVICES

A SC-GRSMC
ROAD SERIES MULTI-CLAMP

B SC-GRSSMC
ROAD SERIES SUPER MULTI-CLAMP

C SC-GRSRA
ROAD SERIES RIGHT ANGLE CLAMP

D SC-GRSSRA
ROAD SERIES STACKABLE RIGHT ANGLE CLAMP

E SC-GRSTL
ROAD SERIES T-LEG CLAMP (part of I)

F SC-670TB
7/8" dia. PEARL™ STYLE TOM MOUNT (not shown)

MOUNTING SYSTEMS

① SC-SBS
SUPER BOOM (small)

② SC-SBM
SUPER BOOM (medium)

③ GPRPT
24" X 24" PERCUSSION TABLE

④ SC-BST
BONGO STAND MOUNT

⑤ LARGE CUSTOM PERCUSSION TABLE
40" X 24"

⑥ SMALL CUSTOM PERCUSSION TABLE
12" X 10"

⑦ LP™ TIMBALE STAND
TOP SECTION ONLY

⑧ SC-SBS24
24" SPANNER BAR (7/8" dia.)

⑨ SC-SB24
24" SPANNER BAR CUT TO 12" (7/8" dia.)

STANDS

◇1 LP™ DOUBLE CONGA STAND
WITH WHEELS

RACK TUBES

I SC-GRSTLA
ROAD SERIES T-LEG ASSEMBLY

II SC-GPR68
68" BAR

III SC-GPR36
36" BAR

IV SC-GPR43.5
43.5" BAR

V SC-GPR59
59" BAR cut to 48"

SET-UP FEATURES:
Plenty of space to move with percussion tables mounted at both ends of the rack. Perfect for live and studio performances. Only one conventional stand insures perfect instrument placement during set-up.

and I cut the whole rack in half, and put things in different places. I'm going to do a Pat Metheny tour next year, and I'm debating how to do this gig. I'm in the process of drawing up a new rack. That's what's great about it. I'm thinking about sitting down on this tour, kind of like more of a jazz thing. So my congas don't have to be on the rack, but everything else could be around me much lower."

Tim "Timbali" Cornwell

TIM "TIMBALI" CORNWELL IS USED TO playing with chart-busters like Babyface and En Vogue, with whom he uses a wide array of hand percussion and electronics. When he first began using a Gibraltar rack on the road with New Edition in 1989, Cornwell employed two separate free-standing racks: one for electronics and the other for acoustic instruments. These days, though, he chooses to use a single cage that surrounds him on stage, from which he mounts a dizzying variety of acoustic and electronic instruments.

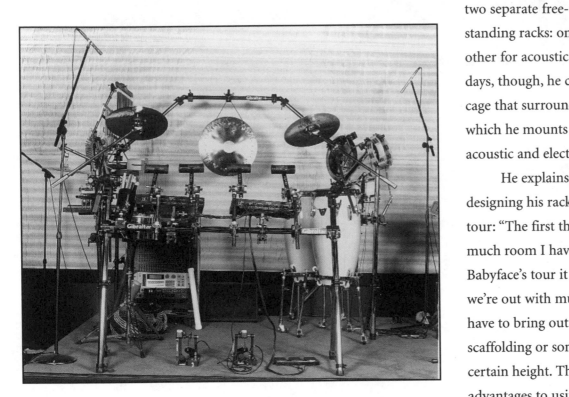

He explains how he goes about designing his rack setup for each new tour: "The first thing I do is find out how much room I have on the stage. On Babyface's tour it was 8' x 8'. And when we're out with multiple acts, they might have to bring out my riser underneath scaffolding or something, so it has to be a certain height. That's one of the biggest advantages to using a rack instead of drum-set hardware: Two people can move a whole wall of stuff in one break between bands.

"Once I've figured out the amount of space I have to work with, then I decide which instruments I'm going to need. For instance, the Babyface gig is predominantly electronics, but he also does a lot of ballads, so I have to make sure that I have a whole wall of really pretty melodic sounds, to make all those ballads sound different. You don't want to

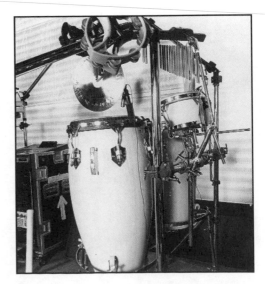

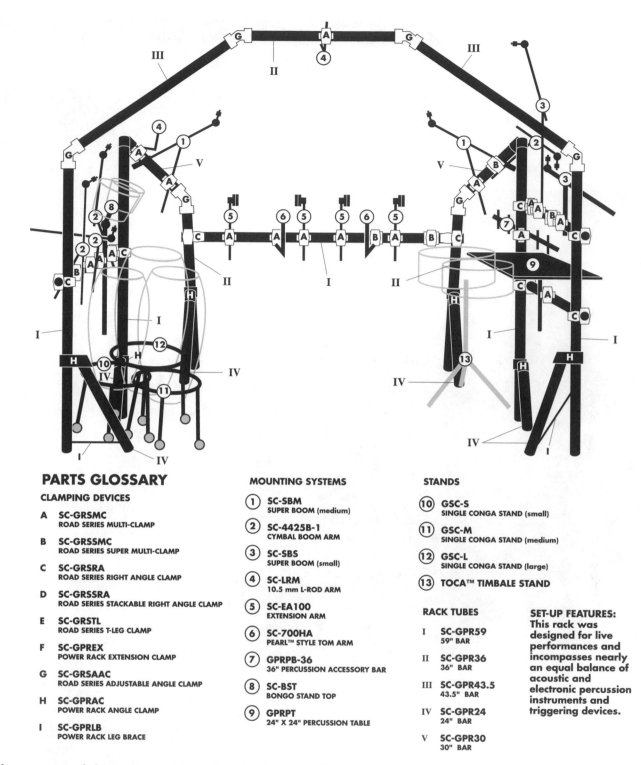

PARTS GLOSSARY

CLAMPING DEVICES

A   **SC-GRSMC**
ROAD SERIES MULTI-CLAMP

B   **SC-GRSSMC**
ROAD SERIES SUPER MULTI-CLAMP

C   **SC-GRSRA**
ROAD SERIES RIGHT ANGLE CLAMP

D   **SC-GRSSRA**
ROAD SERIES STACKABLE RIGHT ANGLE CLAMP

E   **SC-GRSTL**
ROAD SERIES T-LEG CLAMP

F   **SC-GPREX**
POWER RACK EXTENSION CLAMP

G   **SC-GRSAAC**
ROAD SERIES ADJUSTABLE ANGLE CLAMP

H   **SC-GPRAC**
POWER RACK ANGLE CLAMP

I   **SC-GPRLB**
POWER RACK LEG BRACE

MOUNTING SYSTEMS

(1)   **SC-SBM**
SUPER BOOM (medium)

(2)   **SC-4425B-1**
CYMBAL BOOM ARM

(3)   **SC-SBS**
SUPER BOOM (small)

(4)   **SC-LRM**
10.5 mm L-ROD ARM

(5)   **SC-EA100**
EXTENSION ARM

(6)   **SC-700HA**
PEARL™ STYLE TOM ARM

(7)   **GPRPB-36**
36" PERCUSSION ACCESSORY BAR

(8)   **SC-BST**
BONGO STAND TOP

(9)   **GPRPT**
24" X 24" PERCUSSION TABLE

STANDS

(10)   **GSC-S**
SINGLE CONGA STAND (small)

(11)   **GSC-M**
SINGLE CONGA STAND (medium)

(12)   **GSC-L**
SINGLE CONGA STAND (large)

(13)   **TOCA™ TIMBALE STAND**

RACK TUBES

I   **SC-GPR59**
59" BAR

II   **SC-GPR36**
36" BAR

III   **SC-GPR43.5**
43.5" BAR

IV   **SC-GPR24**
24" BAR

V   **SC-GPR30**
30" BAR

SET-UP FEATURES:
This rack was designed for live performances and incompasses nearly an equal balance of acoustic and electronic percussion instruments and triggering devices.

use the same set of chimes on each ballad, so I might have four sets, to set different moods."

Cornwell like to have all of his instruments mounted to the rack, which is why he laughs and says, "I use almost everything Gibraltar makes in that rig." However, there are times when he has to mount his congas and timbales on traditional stands, even though he prefers placing them on the rack. "The drums are actually more stable on the rack. I'm kind of a hard hitter, so I reinforce the rack with a bracket that has two braces on it to keep it from moving anywhere."

F IFTEEN YEARS AGO, BEFORE RACK systems caught the imaginations of consumers, session percussionist Steve Forman built his first rack system from a commercial coat rack, Hollander Speed Rail and galvanized pipe. "It's kind of the nature of percussionists — you improvise," he says. "You begin by building your own instruments, and then you start building your own hardware so that you can use the instruments. It just goes with the territory."

Although his prototypical rack worked well, it also proved to be heavy and cumbersome. After experimenting with a number of other hardware systems, Forman chose a Gibraltar rack. "The kind of work I do as a studio musician requires a completely different setup, not only every day but sometimes every five minutes," he says. "Every time a different cue comes up, it has different instrumentation. All of a sudden I need to have a gong, and then a bell tree, and then something else. So what I need is system which allows me to change instruments immediately. So when I found out about the Gibraltar system with the wide thumb screws, it seemed like a much better thing, and in fact it has

worked out very well."

Although he uses mostly stock Gibraltar parts for both racks, Forman integrates some do-it-yourself elements into his high-tech setups. "I use the big 1-1/2" tubing that the drummers like so much for the bottom of the rack, and

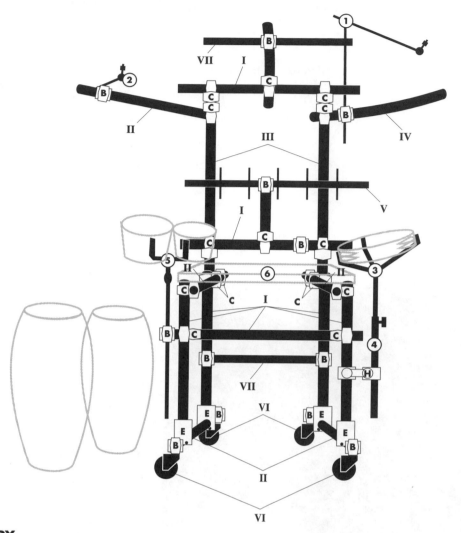

PARTS GLOSSARY

CLAMPING DEVICES

A   **SC-GRSMC**
ROAD SERIES MULTI-CLAMP

B   **SC-GRSSMC**
ROAD SERIES SUPER MULTI-CLAMP

C   **SC-GRSRA**
ROAD SERIES RIGHT ANGLE CLAMP

D   **SC-GRSSRA**
ROAD SERIES STACKABLE RIGHT ANGLE CLAMP

E   **SC-GRSTL**
ROAD SERIES T-LEG CLAMP

H   **SC-SUGC**
SUPER UNIVERSAL GRABBER CLAMP

MOUNTING SYSTEMS

①   **SC-SBS**
SUPER BOOM (small)

②   **SC-CT**
STRAIGHT CYMBAL ARM

③   **GP-0088**
SNARE BASKET

④   **SC-1DEX**
1" dia. TUBE EXTENSION ROD

⑤   **SC-BST**
BONGO STAND TOP

⑥   **GPRPT**
RACK MOUNT PERCUSSION TABLE (24" x 24")

RACK TUBES

I   **SC-GPR30**
30" BAR

II   **SC-GPR24**
24" BAR

III   **SC-GPR36**
36" BAR

IV   **SC-GPR24C**
24" CURVED BAR

V   **SC-GPRPB36**
36" PERCUSSION ACCESSORY BAR

VI   **SC-RC**
RACK CASTERS

VII   **SC-SB36**
36" SPANNER BAR

SET-UP FEATURES:
This rack turns in on itself for easy transport by cartage/tech. company. This rack is not disassembled for transport-cutting set-up time in half.

for any other part that structurally has to hold a lot of weight," he explains. "But wherever I can, I reduce bars down to a 1" tube, so that I can use stock hardware-store spring clamps and loops of cord to hang instruments. Percussion instruments sound so much better and last longer if they're not rigidly attached to things. And if I want to move a small gong, it doesn't take two hands to do it. I can reach up, grab that clamp, and move it from one piece of pipe to the next piece of pipe in less time than it takes to describe it. It works great."

TRIS IMBODEN — WHO BUILT HIS REPUTATION playing with the likes of Chaka Khan and Kenny Loggins — has been using drum racks since 1987. He explains that he had some serious problems with the first one he owned: "I was playing with Jeff Berlin at the time. My tech was in the truck holding the rack up while it was folded with one of the legs still up. Suddenly it came down and almost severed off the tip of his finger. So that wasn't too cool."

Needless to say, Imboden decided to look for a less deadly rack system, and finally settled on his Gibraltar rig. "Traditionally, we drummers have always had trouble positioning things just so, and getting it exactly right where we want it," he says. "Not only has hardware stability and sturdiness progressed in leaps and bounds, but it's also helped us to position instruments. It's a whole other species now, like comparing apples and Chihuahuas. Ten or twenty years ago, you were hard-pressed to get a cymbal stand that would even stand up. And if you were playing with any kind of power, the stand wouldn't last very long."

Imboden has been playing drums with Chicago for many years, and recently discovered an additional advantage to his rack system when the group recorded a big-band album. "The engineers were miking both the top and bottom on the tom-toms," he explains. "They were able to use the mike holders that I had already on the rack to mike the top of the drums. If we had to use floor stands to mike both the top and bottom of the toms, obviously the space would have been limited, with all the drums

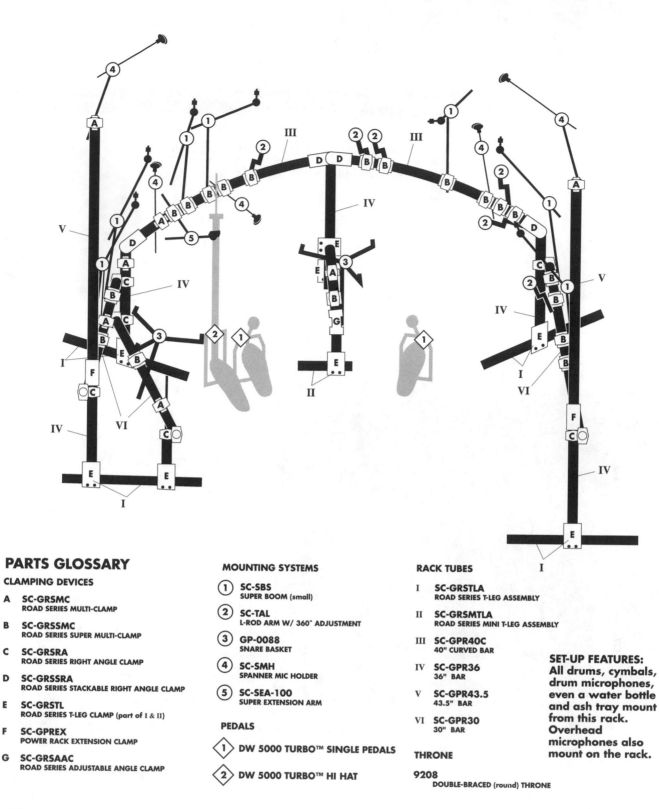

PARTS GLOSSARY

CLAMPING DEVICES

A **SC-GRSMC**
ROAD SERIES MULTI-CLAMP

B **SC-GRSSMC**
ROAD SERIES SUPER MULTI-CLAMP

C **SC-GRSRA**
ROAD SERIES RIGHT ANGLE CLAMP

D **SC-GRSSRA**
ROAD SERIES STACKABLE RIGHT ANGLE CLAMP

E **SC-GRSTL**
ROAD SERIES T-LEG CLAMP (part of I & II)

F **SC-GPREX**
POWER RACK EXTENSION CLAMP

G **SC-GRSAAC**
ROAD SERIES ADJUSTABLE ANGLE CLAMP

MOUNTING SYSTEMS

① **SC-SBS**
SUPER BOOM (small)

② **SC-TAL**
L-ROD ARM W/ 360° ADJUSTMENT

③ **GP-0088**
SNARE BASKET

④ **SC-SMH**
SPANNER MIC HOLDER

⑤ **SC-SEA-100**
SUPER EXTENSION ARM

PEDALS

◇1 DW 5000 TURBO™ SINGLE PEDALS

◇2 DW 5000 TURBO™ HI HAT

RACK TUBES

I **SC-GRSTLA**
ROAD SERIES T-LEG ASSEMBLY

II **SC-GRSMTLA**
ROAD SERIES MINI T-LEG ASSEMBLY

III **SC-GPR40C**
40" CURVED BAR

IV **SC-GPR36**
36" BAR

V **SC-GPR43.5**
43.5" BAR

VI **SC-GPR30**
30" BAR

THRONE

9208
DOUBLE-BRACED (round) THRONE

SET-UP FEATURES:
All drums, cymbals, drum microphones, even a water bottle and ash tray mount from this rack. Overhead microphones also mount on the rack.

that I use.

"I noticed something that Gibraltar came up with that was incredibly innovative," he continues. "Some of the cymbal stands and hi-hat stands have a tripod base that uses something called the ATS system. You can actually put one leg on a surface that is higher or lower than where the other two legs are. We've all played situations where the space was so limited, and you couldn't quite get a cymbal stand in where you wanted it, because you were playing on a drum riser that was too small or something. It's sort of a moot point for me, because I put everything on the rack, but I think it's a very hip idea for drummers who don't use a rack."

Russ McKinnon

LAYING DOWN TIGHTLY PUNCTUATED horn-powered funk with Tower Of Power, Russ McKinnon inhabits one of the most cherished drum chairs in the world. He has to feel confident that his hardware setup will withstand his syncopated grooves, and started using Gibraltar racks two years ago. "I was searching for a very long time to change my setup," he says. "I

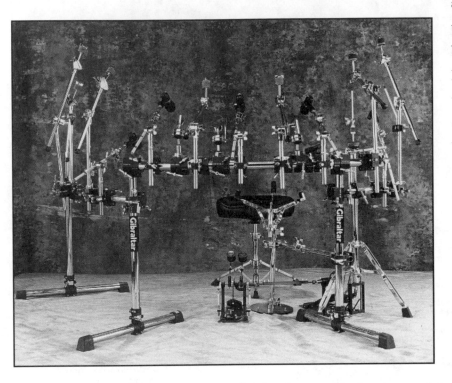

always wanted to mount three rack toms on top of the bass drum, with the middle tom being centered right above the bass drum. No conventional hardware that existed on the planet allowed me to do that. But when Gibraltar came out with those curved rack bars I could finally do it.

"I also wanted to acoustically give the bass drum a break. [With conventional] tom mounts, your average bass drum is supporting around 20 or 30 pounds of wood and metal. You're not allowing the bass drum to do what it wants to do acoustically." By taking stress off of the bass drum, and replacing tripod cymbals bases, floor tom legs and other mounting hardware with clamps, a rack has to stand up under considerable weight and force in order to be effective.

McKinnon estimates that he moves his equipment about 200 times a year, doing clinics and tours with T.O.P. Each time, his entire rig is set up, played, torn down and transported. With such a busy schedule, McKinnon feels that it's important that his kit to be set up correctly every time. "When you have a set as big as mine, it's just a nightmare when you have to fumble

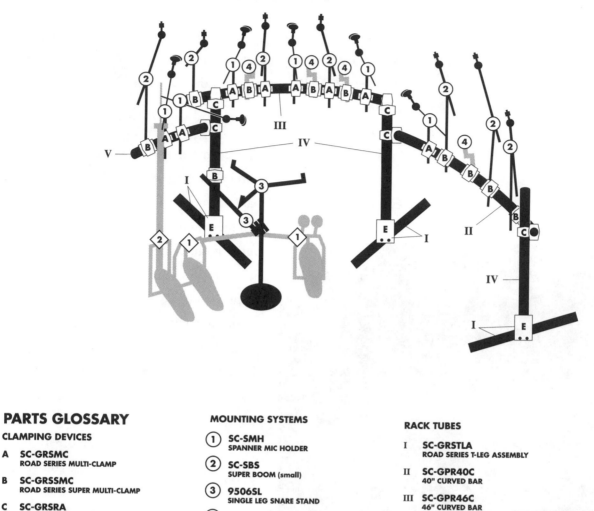

PARTS GLOSSARY

CLAMPING DEVICES

A SC-GRSMC
ROAD SERIES MULTI-CLAMP

B SC-GRSSMC
ROAD SERIES SUPER MULTI-CLAMP

C SC-GRSRA
ROAD SERIES RIGHT ANGLE CLAMP

D SC-GRSSRA
ROAD SERIES STACKABLE RIGHT ANGLE CLAMP

E SC-GRSTL
ROAD SERIES T-LEG CLAMP (part of I)

MOUNTING SYSTEMS

1 SC-SMH
SPANNER MIC HOLDER

2 SC-SBS
SUPER BOOM (small)

3 9506SL
SINGLE LEG SNARE STAND

4 REMO™ TOM ARM

PEDALS

1 DW 5000 TURBO™ DOUBLE PEDAL

2 DW 5000 TURBO™ HI HAT

RACK TUBES

I SC-GRSTLA
ROAD SERIES T-LEG ASSEMBLY

II SC-GPR40C
40" CURVED BAR

III SC-GPR46C
46" CURVED BAR

IV SC-GPR30
30" BAR

V SC-GPR24C
24" CURVED BAR

THRONE

RSGMC
GIBRALTAR THRONE SEAT by ROC-N-SOC™

SC-0037
DOUBLE-BRACED THRONE BASE

SET-UP FEATURES:
All drums, cymbals and microphones are mounted from this rack. Hi-hat is also mounted to the rack which helps insure exact pedal positioning.

around with stands and memory clamps," he says. "Consistency's the name of the game because everything locks right into place with my rack. I can walk in and begin my job of playing, instead of having to be my own drum tech."

Making full use of his hardware system, McKinnon even mounts his drum microphones on his rack. "I don't know why more people don't take advantage of that. It really creates a clean setup, because there's nothing on the floor in front of you. I have microphone mounts for every drum and darn near every cymbal, but when you look at the kit it doesn't look busy. If I was to use conventional microphone stands with the exact same kit it would look like a junk store back there."

Jonathan Moffett

LONG BEFORE GIBRALTAR WAS EVEN A twinkle in the eye of the Kaman corporation, Jonathan Moffett designed his very first rack to take on the road with the Jacksons' ground-breaking Victory tour. "I heard from the Jackson brothers that it was going to be the biggest musical event and concert tour that had ever gone out, and they wanted to make an extravaganza out of it," he remembers. "And I wanted to be a part of it visually as well as musically." Having studied commercial art and drumming with equal enthusiasm in his youth, Moffett saw an opportunity to make use of both of his talents at once. He designed a massive rack using thick curved tubing, which had previously never been done at that time. The Jackson organization had to commission two separate companies to build it, at a cost of $13,000. "There's a mystery going on about that rack," Moffett confides, "because it's missing, and nobody knows where it is. Each individual Jackson brother hit me up at a different time on the tour and wanted that rack. It went to their storage, and then it was shipped out and was displayed at the '85 NAMM show in Anaheim. Then it went back in storage and has never been seen again."

Since then, Moffett has made a personal statement with his setup every time he goes out on the road. He designed the rack that he used on the 1994 Janet Jackson tour with the

"They saw my drawing of the rack and got obsessed with it. I kept telling them that I thought it was going to need more custom pieces than they had to work with, and they'd say ' Yeah, but let's see just how far we can go.'"

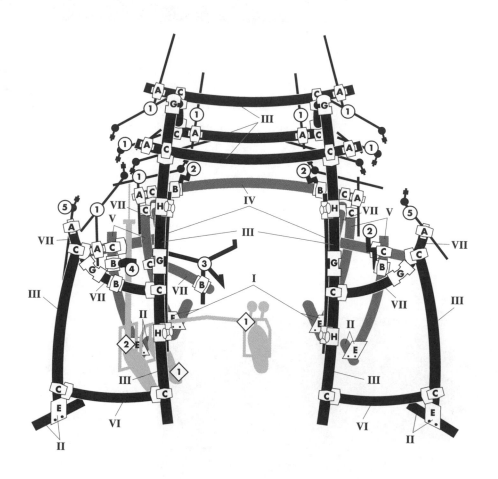

PARTS GLOSSARY

CLAMPING DEVICES

A   **SC-GRSMC**
ROAD SERIES MULTI-CLAMP

B   **SC-GRSSMC**
ROAD SERIES SUPER MULTI-CLAMP

C   **SC-GRSRA**
ROAD SERIES RIGHT ANGLE CLAMP

D   **SC-GRSSRA**
ROAD SERIES STACKABLE RIGHT ANGLE CLAMP

E   **SC-GRSTL**
ROAD SERIES T-LEG CLAMP (part of I & II)

F   **SC-GPREX**
POWER RACK EXTENSION CLAMP

G   **SC-GRSAAC**
ROAD SERIES ADJUSTABLE ANGLE CLAMP

H   **SC-SUGC**
SUPER UNIVERSAL GRABBER CLAMP

MOUNTING SYSTEMS

①   **SC-SBS**
SUPER BOOM (small)

②   **SC-TAL**
L-ROD ARM W/ 360° ADJUSTMENT

③   **GP-0088**
SNARE BASKET

④   **SC-SEA100**
SUPER EXTENSION ARM

⑤   **SC-CT**
STRAIGHT CYMBAL ARM

PEDALS

◇1   DW 5000™ TURBO DOUBLE PEDAL

◇2   DW 5000™ TURBO HI HAT

RACK TUBES

I   **SC-GRSTLA**
ROAD SERIES T-LEG ASSEMBLY

II   **SC-GRSMTLA**
ROAD SERIES MINI T-LEG ASSEMBLY

III   **SC-GPR40C**
40" CURVED BAR

IV   **SC-GPR46C**
46" CURVED BAR

V   **SC-GPR40C cut to 36"**
36" CURVED BAR

VI   **SC-GPR40C cut to 30"**
30" CURVED BAR

VII   **SC-GPR24**
24" CURVED BAR

SET-UP FEATURES:
Nicknamed "The Thunderdome" Jonathan's creation is not only unique-it's functional. All drums and cymbals are mounted from the rack. Assembly and transport was fairly easy with a set-up time of 45 minutes. All parts were marked and coded for quick assembly.

help of Gibraltar's West Coast representatives. "They wouldn't give up on it," Moffett says. "They saw my drawing of the rack and got obsessed with it. I kept telling them that I thought it was going to need more custom pieces than they had to work with, and they'd say 'Yeah, but let's see just how far we can go.' By the time we finished it looked practically just like the drawing. I was very satisfied and gratified by their dedication to make this thing happen."

JOE PORCARO HAS A UNIQUE PERSPECTIVE ON the business of drumming. He raised a family as a professional drummer in the fertile Los Angeles session scene during the '50s, '60s and '70s. One of his sons, the late Jeff Porcaro, followed in his dad's footsteps and became the quintessential rock session drummer from the '70s to the early '90s. Today, Joe Porcaro remains active in the studios and clubs around L.A., and

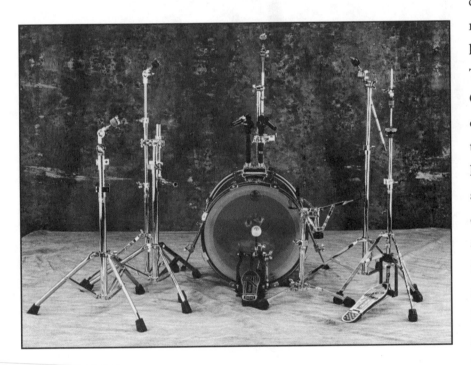

continues to pass his knowledge on to new generations of drummers as the head of the Percussion Institute of Technology in Hollywood, California. Considering his longevity, it should come as little surprise that Porcaro is a traditionalist when it comes to his hardware setup. "I don't use a rack," he says. "I have one that I use for electronics, but I haven't used that in ages. Maybe down the road I'll get one for studio work." Despite his nonchalant attitude about using rack systems, Porcaro is very particular about his stands and pedals.

"I like to feel that I have something really solid underneath — the foot pedal, the hi-hat, the stands — so that nothing topples over," he says. "As far as the bass pedal and the hi-hat, I like something that's nice and free, but not too free. Paul Humphries, the drummer who I used to work with on the Glen Campbell show, taught me

something that I remember to this day. He said that you can check out five or ten hi-hat stands from the same company, and they're all different. I always used to go to the store, buy a new hi-hat stand and go home with it, thinking, 'Wow, I

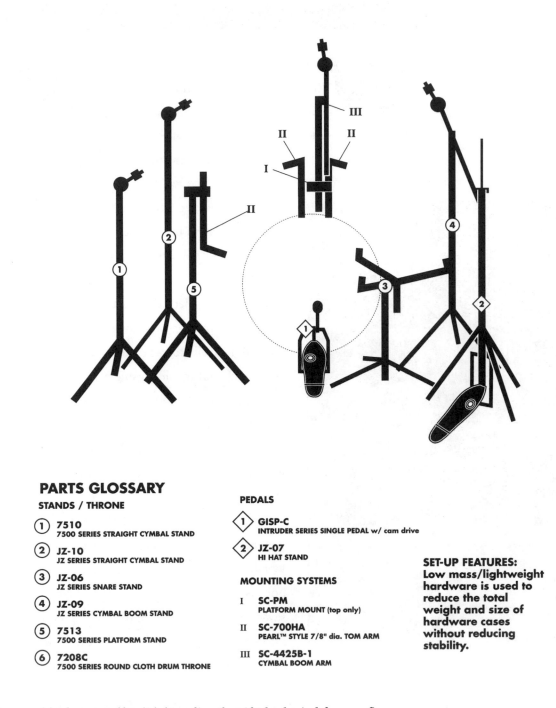

PARTS GLOSSARY

STANDS / THRONE

1. **7510**
   7500 SERIES STRAIGHT CYMBAL STAND

2. **JZ-10**
   JZ SERIES STRAIGHT CYMBAL STAND

3. **JZ-06**
   JZ SERIES SNARE STAND

4. **JZ-09**
   JZ SERIES CYMBAL BOOM STAND

5. **7513**
   7500 SERIES PLATFORM STAND

6. **7208C**
   7500 SERIES ROUND CLOTH DRUM THRONE

PEDALS

1. **GISP-C**
   INTRUDER SERIES SINGLE PEDAL w/ cam drive

2. **JZ-07**
   HI HAT STAND

MOUNTING SYSTEMS

I **SC-PM**
  PLATFORM MOUNT (top only)

II **SC-700HA**
  PEARL™ STYLE 7/8" dia. TOM ARM

III **SC-4425B-1**
  CYMBAL BOOM ARM

SET-UP FEATURES:
Low mass/lightweight hardware is used to reduce the total weight and size of hardware cases without reducing stability.

copped a good hi-hat stand.' I didn't realize that if I had tried four or five more hi-hats made by the same company I would have found an even better one. But I think that might be different today."

Porcaro admits that drum and cymbal stands are built more heavy-duty than they were years ago, but never felt a need for the additional weight and bulkiness. "Of course, today's cymbal stands are directed at mainly the rock drummers," he says. "That was kind of forced on you for a while there. You'd go to buy a cymbal stand and that's all there was. For what I do, I don't need that heavy, bulky stuff. But Gibraltar came out with new light-weight stands, which have smaller-diameter tubing, but it's still sturdy. I'm using those when I play clubs, and I want to start using them in the studios too."

WHILE PLAYING PERCUSSION WITH THE Rippingtons, Steve Reid has used Gibraltar racks practically since the company's inception. "Gibraltar hooked me up with their very first rack system," he says, "which was much different than it is now." From

that first modest setup, Reid's hardware system has evolved into a cage which nearly envelops him with a diverse assortment of instruments.

Clearly not affected by claustrophobia, Reid explains, "Since the rack encompasses me all the way around, I'm able to get to all of my instruments in a very quick and musically effective way. I've got two tiers and a couple tables that make a third level. I can play two or three things at once without having to really twist my body around. That's something I wouldn't have been able to do with any other kind of hardware."

Logging as many as 150 days per year on tour, Reid depends on his hardware to be strong and road-worthy. "I have a reputation for breaking little cymbal booms and tilters because they weren't heavy duty," he says. "People will give me stuff to try, because they know I'm going to beat the heck out of it. The old stuff wasn't nearly as strong as it is now. The new round bars really will support a lot of weight, and I play very hard with my hands."

Reid continues to experiment with his setup. He has recently added a three-tiered cymbal arm, and

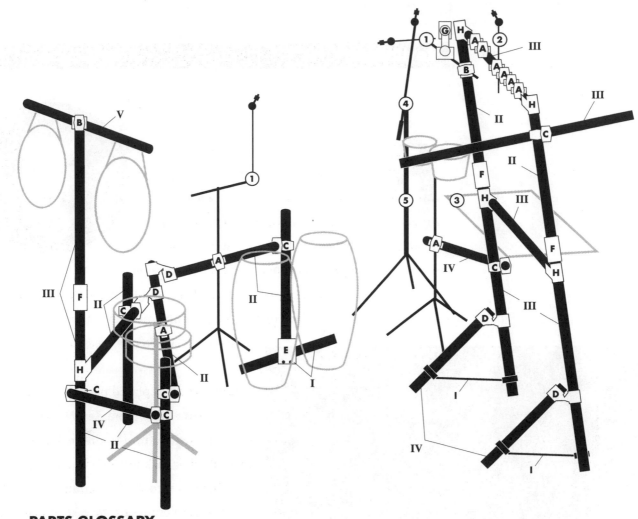

PARTS GLOSSARY

CLAMPING DEVICES

A SC-GRSMC
ROAD SERIES MULTI-CLAMP

B SC-GRSSMC
ROAD SERIES SUPER MULTI-CLAMP

C SC-GRSRA
ROAD SERIES RIGHT ANGLE CLAMP

D SC-GPRAC
POWER RACK ANGLE CLAMP

E SC-GRSTL
ROAD SERIES T-LEG CLAMP (part of I)

F SC-GPREX
POWER RACK EXTENSION CLAMP

G SC-SUGC
SUPER UNIVERSAL GRABBER CLAMP

H SC-GPRTC
POWER RACK T-CLAMP

I SC-GPRLB
POWER RACK LEG BRACE

MOUNTING SYSTEMS

① SC-4425B-1
CYMBAL BOOM ARM

② SC-CT
STRAIGHT CYMBAL ARM

③ CUSTOM PERCUSSION TABLE
(30" X 22")

STANDS

④ 9509M
MEDIUM BOOM STAND

⑤ 9516
BONGO STAND

RACK TUBES

I SC-GRSTLA
ROAD SERIES T-LEG ASSEMBLY

II SC-GPR30
30" BAR

III SC-GPR43.5
43.5" BAR

IV SC-GPR24
24" BAR

V SC-SB36
36" SPANNER BAR (1" dia.)

SET-UP FEATURES
Multiple sound effects "hanging racks" creating several individual percussion workstations for traditional Afro-Cuban instruments and unique sound effects.

has begun to use two Gibraltar Intruder pedals to play cowbell and woodblock with his feet. "That's something new that I brought out on this tour," he says. "I'm trying to work both feet independently, while playing congas and timbales and toys with my hands. It's been a lot of fun. I prefer having the congas sit on the ground, because I like the tone of them on the wood. So when I'm sitting I can play two pedals at once, and when I'm standing up I have one pedal by the timbales and one by the bongo."

HAVING RECENTLY GOTTEN MARRIED, percussionist Kevin Ricard found himself clearing out the old junk from his garage "to make room for *my wife's* old junk," he jokes. "I found cymbal stands and pieces of hardware from years ago when I first started playing. Along the years it's sort of piled up over there, and I noticed how much the quality has improved since then. The tightening mechanisms and the cymbal attachments are so much easier to work with now."

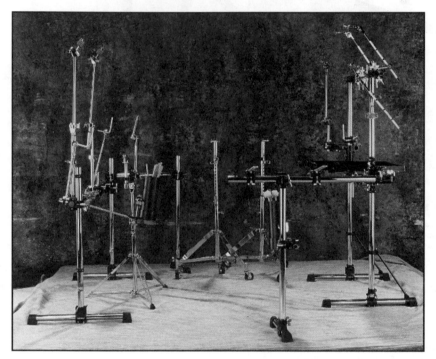

Ricard, who has played percussion with the likes of Bette Midler and Kenny Loggins, made the switch from traditional hardware to a Gibraltar rack in 1993, when Loggins was about to record a live album and a video. "I did it just because of the ease of placement that a rack offers," he explains. "Loggins is very into percussion, and he wanted a lot of drums available for different sounds and colors, and the rack made it easier to put stuff where I needed it."

Ricard rarely alters his percussion setup, although he occasionally incorporates electronic trigger pads, which he attaches to the top bars of his rack "so that it's easy to get in and out without drastically changing my setup." However, before he owned his first rack system, Ricard was asked to play djembes and bata drums with Loggins. "At the time, there were no stands for them," he says. "I ended up using wooden stands, but they weren't nearly as stable as the newer

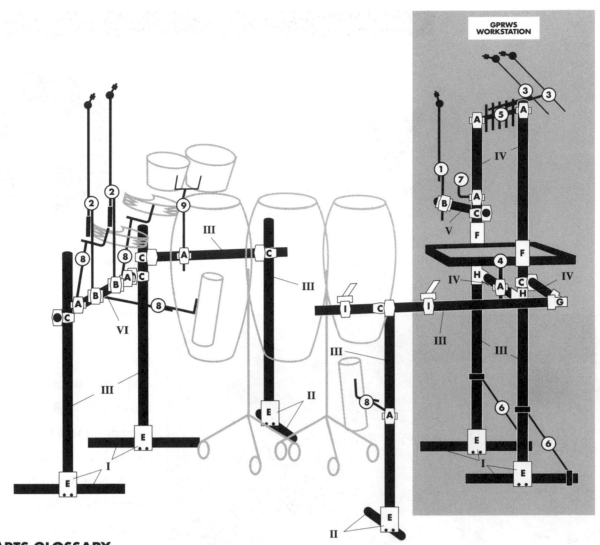

PARTS GLOSSARY

CLAMPING DEVICES

A   **SC-GRSMC**
ROAD SERIES MULTI-CLAMP

B   **SC-GRSSMC**
ROAD SERIES SUPER MULTI-CLAMP

C   **SC-GRSRA**
ROAD SERIES RIGHT ANGLE CLAMP

D   **SC-GRSSRA**
ROAD SERIES STACKABLE RIGHT ANGLE CLAMP

E   **SC-GRSTL**
ROAD SERIES T-LEG CLAMP (part of I)

F   **SC-GPREX**
POWER RACK EXTENSION CLAMP

G   **SC-GRSAAC**
ROAD SERIES ADJUSTABLE ANGLE CLAMP

H   **SC-GPRTC**
POWER RACK T-CLAMP

I   **SC-GPREC**
POWER RACK ELECTRONIC CLAMP

MOUNTING SYSTEMS

①   **SC-SBS**
SUPER BOOM (small)

②   **SC-SBM**
SUPER BOOM (medium)

③   **SC-MB**
MINI BOOM

④   **GPRPT**
24" X 24" PERCUSSION TABLE

⑤   **GPRPB-36**
36" PERCUSSION ACCESSORY BAR

⑥   **GPRLB**
POWER RACK LEG BRACE

⑦   **SC-SLR**
SUPER L-ROD

⑧   **SC-4425D-1**
COWBELL/TOM ARM

⑨   **SC-BST**
BONGO STAND TOP

RACK TUBES

I   **SC-GRSTLA**
ROAD SERIES T-LEG ASSEMBLY

II   **SC-GRSMTLA**
ROAD SERIES MINI T-LEG ASSEMBLY

III   **SC-GPR43.5**
43.5" BAR

IV   **SC-GPR30**
30" BAR

V   **SC-GPR24**
24" BAR

VI   **SC-GPR59**
59" BAR

SET-UP FEATURES:

This set-up is designed for live performances. It allows the percussionist to move freely within the set-up and exit from the front or rear facilitating access to any point on the stage for featured solos etc.

stands. And now you can mount a djembe on a conga stand, which is awfully convenient. These days they're taking into account that there are percussionists who want to use hardware, and they're creating things that make it easier to mount little cowbells and tambourines and blocks into your setup."

Van Romaine

VAN ROMAINE IS A BLUR OF MOTION ON stage with the Steve Morse Band, navigating his way through a complex fusion of instrumental rock, jazz and bluegrass. Although any drummer would admire his lightning speed and powerful chops, few might realize that Romaine once had to pay dearly for them before he began using a Gibraltar rack system in 1990.

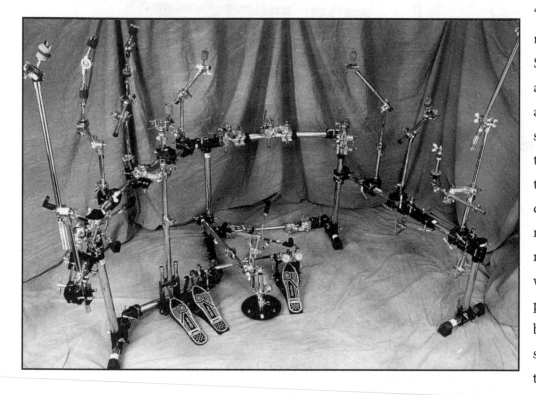

"It was about four or five months into my work with Steve Morse," he says. "First of all, I have a huge drum set, and even though we'd have the same drum tech for a tour, they would often change from tour to tour. With multiple drum techs working for us, none of them ever quite set up my drum set exactly the right way. The only way to get it perfect was to go out myself before the set and readjust the snare drum stand, pedals, floor toms and cymbals.

"Also, the Morse band's dynamics get loud a lot of times — it's really a hard-hitting kind of thing. All of my old hardware was constantly moving around and would take up a lot of space on stage before I switched to the rack. We tend to play in a lot of different situations, so just eliminating the tripod legs cut

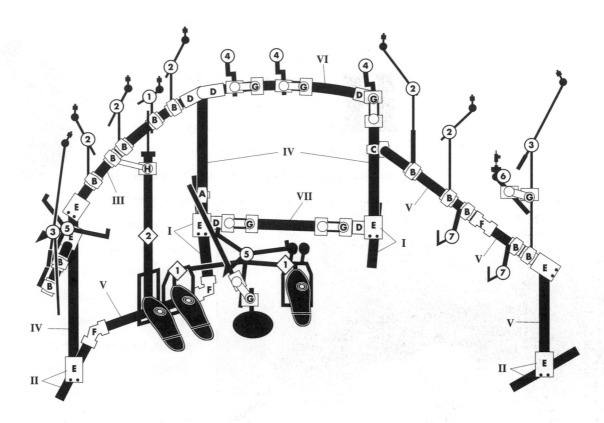

PARTS GLOSSARY

CLAMPING DEVICES

A **SC-GRSMC**
ROAD SERIES MULTI-CLAMP

B **SC-GRSSMC**
ROAD SERIES SUPER MULTI-CLAMP

C **SC-GRSRA**
ROAD SERIES RIGHT ANGLE CLAMP

D **SC-GRSSRA**
ROAD SERIES STACKABLE RIGHT ANGLE CLAMP

E **SC-GRSTL**
ROAD SERIES T-LEG CLAMP (part of I)

F **SC-GRSAAC**
ROAD SERIES ADJUSTABLE ANGLE CLAMP

G **SC-SUGC**
SUPER UNIVERSAL GRABBER CLAMP

H **SC-SEA-100**
SUPER EXTENSION ARM

MOUNTING SYSTEMS

① **SC-4425B-1**
CYMBAL BOOM ARM

② **SC-SBS**
SUPER BOOM (small)

③ **SC-SBM**
SUPER BOOM (medium)

④ **SC-TAL**
L-ROD ARM W/ 360° ADJUSTMENT

⑤ **9506SL**
SINGLE LEG SNARE STAND

⑥ **9507X**
FIXED HI HAT CYMBAL MOUNT

⑦ **SC-4425D-1**
TOM/COWBELL ARM

PEDALS

① **GIDP-S**
INTRUDER SERIES DOUBLE PEDAL w/ sprocket drive

② **9507NL**
9500 SERIES NO-LEG HI HAT

RACK TUBES

I **SC-GRSTLA**
ROAD SERIES T-LEG ASSEMBLY

II **SC-GRSMTLA**
ROAD SERIES MINI T-LEG ASSEMBLY

III **SC-GPR40C**
40" CURVED BAR

IV **SC-GPR36**
36" BAR

V **SC-GPR24**
24" BAR

VI **SC-GPR40C cut to 36"**
36" CURVED BAR

VII **SC-SB24**
24" SPANNER BAR

THRONE

9208
DOUBLE-BRACED (round) THRONE

SET-UP FEATURES:
Pedals are held in place by the rack. This eliminates any pedal movement and guarantees exact pedal placement during set-up.

down on a lot of space and made the setup a lot tighter."

Using a Gibraltar system, Romaine is able to mount practically his entire setup to the rack, including his floor toms, pedals and snare stand. With Morse he uses a double bass kit, and says that Gibraltar's legless hi-hat and rack-mounted single-leg snare stand have made pedal setup much easier. "I tend to have my double pedals pretty close together, so it's nice not to have the hi-hat and snare stand tripods to contend with."

HEAVY METAL VETERAN BOBBY RONDINELLI thoroughly understands the importance of having strong, durable hardware. While drumming with bands such as Rainbow, Quiet Riot and Warlock, as well as his current gig with Black Sabbath, Rondinelli plays with a ferocious attack, and is constantly putting his gear to the test.

Before he started using a rack, Rondinelli clamped his cymbal stands to the drum riser in order to prevent them from falling over. "I used to have a guy standing by just to pick up cymbal stands and put them back up," he says. But then he began to use a Gibraltar rack in 1992, and reports that stability is no longer a problem, since there's so much weight on his rack. "I wanted to use three toms in the front, with the center tom directly in line with the snare drum," he says. "I didn't want two toms on the right bass drum and one on the left. It seemed like the most logical thing to do, and certainly has made my life a lot easier."

In addition to the rack system, Rondinelli feels that the double-bass drum pedal "is the best thing that came along for drummers in the last 50 years, because you don't have to lug a second bass drum

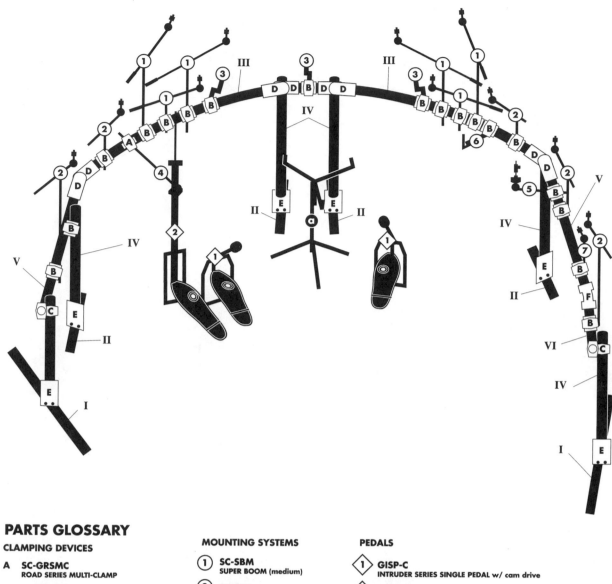

PARTS GLOSSARY

CLAMPING DEVICES

A   SC-GRSMC
ROAD SERIES MULTI-CLAMP

B   SC-GRSSMC
ROAD SERIES SUPER MULTI-CLAMP

C   SC-GRSRA
ROAD SERIES RIGHT ANGLE CLAMP

D   SC-GRSSRA
ROAD SERIES STACKABLE RIGHT ANGLE CLAMP

E   SC-GRSTL
ROAD SERIES T-LEG CLAMP (part of I)

F   SC-GRSAAC
ROAD SERIES ADJUSTABLE ANGLE CLAMP

MOUNTING SYSTEMS

①   SC-SBM
SUPER BOOM (medium)

②   SC-SBS
SUPER BOOM (small)

③   SC-TAL
L-ROD ARM W/ 360° ADJUSTMENT

④   SC-SEA-100
SUPER EXTENSION ARM

⑤   9507X
FIXED HI HAT CYMBAL MOUNT

⑥   SC-4425D-1
TOM/COWBELL ARM

⑦   SC-CT
STRAIGHT CYMBAL ARM

PEDALS

◇1   GISP-C
INTRUDER SERIES SINGLE PEDAL w/ cam drive

◇2   9507NL
9500 SERIES NO-LEG HI HAT

RACK TUBES

I   SC-GRSTLA
ROAD SERIES T-LEG ASSEMBLY

II   SC-GRSMTLA
ROAD SERIES MINI T-LEG ASSEMBLY

III   SC-GPR40C
40" CURVED BAR

IV   SC-GPR36
36" BAR

V   SC-GPR42.5 cut to 40"
40" BAR

VI   SC-GPR24
24" BAR

STANDS / THRONE

ⓐ   9506
SNARE STAND

9208S
SHORT DRUM THRONE

SET-UP FEATURES:
Easy access to all drums and cymbals on kit, with uniform height and width of key cymbals and toms.

everywhere. If I'm touring I always use the big double-bass kit, but I use the double pedal for any local gigs or sessions. I started using it about five years ago, and found that I was able to play single strokes more quickly with a double pedal than I could with two separate bass drums. It's like if you were to play a single-stroke roll on two different tom toms, it's harder to play it really fast and clean than it would be if you were playing it on one drum."

CHAPTER 4

HARDWARE MAINTENANCE AND REPAIR

When it comes to equipment maintenance and repair, there are two types of drummers. Some are meticulous with their gear, methodically lubricating every moving part, searching for flecks of dust, earnestly polishing. Others are perhaps the more stereotypical drummers, proudly displaying the stains and scratches on their equipment like hard-earned battle scars. No matter which kind of drummer you are, it's important to know how to perform at least a few basic hardware repairs and maintenance tips in order to be competitive.

Even if you feel ambivalent about the appearance of your kit, you simply cannot ignore the condition of your drums. You can have the best technique and flashiest moves on the planet, but you still won't be able to get a gig unless you also sound good. Although fresh drumheads and mirror-smooth bearing edges play a vital role in attaining a satisfactory drum sound, a rattling lug or squeaky pedal can effectively nullify the world's best edges and heads.

Use your eyes and ears to determine the condition of your hardware. If your pedal squeaks or a stand gets wobbly, it's time to take a closer look at what's going on.

Maintenance

Although it is impossible to entirely avoid emergency hardware problems, you can prevent many of them by practicing a few common-sense maintenance tips. First of all, use your eyes and ears to determine the condition of your hardware. If your pedal squeaks or a stand gets wobbly, it's time to take a closer look at what's going on. Here are a few suggested maintenance routines that might take some time to perform, but can save you money, as well as embarrassment.

Resist Rust. Not only is rust an unsightly nuisance, but it can also render a piece of hardware useless by freezing moving parts in place. Rust is created when your hardware is exposed to moisture for a prolonged period of time. So whenever any kind of fluid spills on your equipment, wipe it off as soon as you can with a dry cloth, and always store your gear in a warm, dry place.

Don't use rust remover if rust should develop on a piece of hardware. Although it will take off rust very nicely, it also does an equally good job of removing chrome-plating from stands. Your only option for combating rust is to scrape it off with a piece of steel wool, which, unfortunately, will also leave small scrapes on the chrome.

Of course, your best bet is to be as prepared as you can by regularly polishing your hardware. There are polishes on the market that are specifically designed for drum-set hardware, although there are a number of commercial metal polishes that will work equally well. Not only will polish keep your stands in a pristine condition, but it also seals them with a moisture-resistant coating.

Keep It Lubed. If you play loud and rarely amplify your drums, you might not even know whether or not your pedals squeak. But you certainly will find out as soon as you go into a recording studio or do a gig where your drums are miked. The sound of squeaky pedals through P.A. speakers is reminiscent of fingernails scraping a blackboard, and can make even the greatest drumming unbearable. Therefore, it's a good idea to regularly lubricate all the moving parts on your pedals with some form of petroleum- or even vegetable-based oil. But why stop with your pedals? Lubricating all the moving parts of your hardware — retractable tripod legs, wing bolts, even your drum throne — makes setting-up and tearing-down easier, and extends the life of your equipment.

Spares To Spare. Any piece of drum-set hardware actually is a collection of parts that are welded, bolted or clamped to one another. Even the most insignificant-looking wingscrew or spring can cause deceptively large problems if you allow it to wear out to the point of breaking. Remember, if something goes wrong with your equipment while you're on a gig, your professionalism will be measured by how quickly and efficiently you deal with it. So head-off small problems before they develop into bigger ones. For example, you should immediately replace cymbal felts and plastic cymbal sleeves when they start to show signs of wear. Otherwise you'll allow metal parts of your stands to gouge into the cymbals, irreparably damaging them. And check the condition of the springs, beater nut and beater of your bass drum pedals to avoid losing the use your bass drum in the middle of a song.

It's wise to carry with you a spare snare drum and bass drum pedal whenever you are working professionally. If you break a tom head, hi-hat or even a cymbal, you can usually re-orchestrate your drum parts in such a way that the audience probably won't even notice that you have problem. But if you suddenly lose the use of your snare or bass drum, and don't have a spare, you practically can't continue playing — at least not without sounding like a complete dork. And even if you have a spare snare head or bass drumhead, you'll still have to stop playing for at least ten minutes or so while you fumble around changing heads.

Still, it's a good idea to have an extra full set of heads, as well as a roll of duct tape, some form of lubrication for your pedals, at least two drum keys, a screwdriver, a wrench, spare snare strands, snare tape or string, extra tension rods and washers, a spare bass drum beater, a second hi-hat clutch, an extra bass pedal strap or chain, a second bass drum hoop guard, a double-pedal anchor, Velcro strips to help hold your stands and pedals in place, a clean cloth rag and cymbal felts. Admittedly, not every drummer can afford all this spare stuff, or has a large-enough car to lug it around. So try to choose the spare parts that you will most likely need, based on your style of playing and the quality of your equipment.

The Value Of Cases. Though it might just seem like an unwelcome, additional expense after you've laid-down your hard-earned cash on a new kit, a full set of drum cases is one of the best investments you can make. Cases will not only protect your equipment from moisture, scratches and *dings*, but will also extend the life of your kit, make it infinitely easier to carry and store and actually will allow you to sell it down-the-line for a higher price when you want to upgrade to a better set.

There are a number of available case options for hardware. Flight cases offer the best protection, and feature solid wood sides, internal padding, casters, heavy-duty retractable handles and a removable or hinged top that is locked-down with latches. Unfortunately, flight cases are also rather bulky and impractical for drummers who mostly play local club gigs. For them, a trap case is the most practical and perhaps the most standard hardware case one can find. Trap cases usually have fiberboard sides, a wood base, casters, retractable handles and a removable top that is held by straps. Your next best bet is a soft hardware case, which usually has padded vinyl sides, a zippered top and vinyl handle straps. But even if you can't afford a soft bag, you should still go to an Army surplus store and pick up a duffel bag for a few dollars to throw your hardware into. Your back and your gear will thank you for it.

Emergency Repair

No matter how prepared you might be, you can't avoid Murphy's Law. Sooner or later some stand or pedal is going to break without warning, and you'll have to do some pretty fancy footwork to salvage your gig. Although a quick wit and sense of spontaneity will probably best serve you while under such duress, here are a few common on-stage disasters that you can prepare for — and undoubtedly will one day face — with short-term solutions for emergency repairs, and long-term solutions for a more permanent fix.

Tensioning Hardware

Noisy Lugs. There was a time when almost all drum lugs contained a metal spring insert that was the scourge of most drum-set players. Drummers who weren't aware of this could literally go nuts trying to discover the source of the weird boinging sound that the springs made when the drum was struck. Fortunately, most modern drum companies have replaced the spring with a plastic or vinyl tube insert, eliminating the problem altogether. Still, there are plenty of older drum sets out there, as well as new, cheap, entry-level kits that employ the older lug design.

Short-Term Repair: Unfortunately, there is none.

Long-Term Repair: You will have to disassemble each boinging drum, so be careful to keep track of all the loose screws, tension rods and washers. Remove the tension rods, hoops and heads from the drum. Unscrew each lug from the inside of the shell. Stuff the inner cavity of the lug with cotton or cloth so that it surrounds the spring insert, and reattach the lug to the shell. Replace the heads, hoops and tension rods once every lug has been stuffed.

Stripped Tension Rods & Lug Receptor. You will know that either your tension rod or the lug's rod receptor is stripped when you are unable to make the rod grip the corresponding lug's receptor. Be prepared to do a little investigative work to determine the problem.

Short-Term Repair: Remove the tension rod and inspect it to see if its teeth are stripped. If you have a spare rod, replace the stripped rod and re-tune the drum. If the rod appears to be intact, the problem resides inside the lug. In that case, tune the drum the best you can, and try to avoid hitting it altogether.

Long-Term Repair: Replace the rod if it is stripped. Replace the lug if its rod receptor is stripped.

Pedals

Squeaky Hi-Hat Pedal. If your hi-hat is squeaking, you can probably just follow the same procedure you would take with a squeaky bass pedal by lubricating its moving parts. However, the squeak can also result from a bent pull rod that is scraping against the inside of the stand.

Short-Term Repair: Remove both cymbals, the upper tier of the hi-hat stand and the upper pull rod. If the pull rod appears to be bent, try to bend it back into shape. Reassemble the stand and continue to play.

Long-Term Repair: Replace the upper pull rod with a new one.

Weak Bass Pedal Response. It can be especially embarrassing on-stage when your bass beater suddenly doesn't spring back quickly enough, or not at all.

Short-Term Repair: There are a couple of potential culprits for a non-responsive pedal. First check to see if the nut which holds the spring to the pedal has either loosened considerably or has come off entirely. If this is the case, replace and/or tighten the nut and continue playing. On the other hand, if the spring seems to have lost its suppleness or has broken, you must replace the spring. If you don't have a replacement with you, you simply will have to suffer through the gig.

Long-Term Repair: Regularly check your bass pedal springs and replace them when necessary.

Weak Hi-Hat Pedal Response. This can especially be a problem for drummers who play hard and loud. Fortunately, you can usually make it to the end of a song, or even to the end of a set if necessary, without the audience knowing that something went wrong.

Short-Term Repair: Most likely, the upper pull rod of your hi-hat has unscrewed from the bottom pull rod. Remove both hi-hat cymbals, and the upper tier of your hi-hat stand. Reinstall the upper pull rod, replace the stand's upper tier and both cymbals, and continue playing. If your upper pull rod is fine when you inspect it, chances are that you actually broke the metal strip or chain which connects the footboard to the lower pull rod. The best short-term repair is to try to reconnect the strip or chain using duct tape or even Super Glue in order to make it through the gig.

Long-Term Repair: If you've broken a metal part, take the stand to your local drum shop and have an expert repair it.

Stripped Hi-Hat Clutch. Your clutch has one screw which holds the clutch to the pull rod and another which holds your top cymbal to the clutch. If either becomes stripped, the net result is that your top cymbal can't be attached to the stand.

Short-Term Repair: If you don't have a spare clutch, you will have to jerry-rig the cymbal onto the upper pull rod. Tear off a long piece of duct tape, and then tear that piece of tape down the middle, so that you have two skinny, long strips of tape. Circle the pull rod with one of the strips of tape until it forms a lip that is wide enough to hold the top cymbal in place. Put the cymbal on top of the lip and circle the area directly above the cymbal with the other strip of tape, attempting to hold the cymbal as firmly as possible.

Long-Term Repair: Replace the clutch.

Excessive Footboard Movement. If your bass or hi-hat pedal footboard suddenly begins moving from side-to-side while you're playing, you should first check to see if the Y-shaped radius rod which is attached to the bottom of the pedal's heel plate has disconnected itself from the pedal's frame. If so, simply reconnect it and continue to play. If not, you've got a bigger problem on your hands — the radius rod has probably broken off of the footboard.

Short-Term Repair: Duct tape the pedal's heel plate to the floor and continue playing.

Long-Term Repair: Either the radius rod needs to be re-welded to the heel-plate, or an entirely new footboard needs to be installed. Take the pedal to your local drum shop and have it repaired by an expert.

Stands

Stripped Screws. As screws are repeatedly used, dirt and grime build up in their threads, which eventually can cause the screw to become increasingly difficult to turn. In this condition, it can be easy to strip a screw, and two diametrically opposite problems will occur: either the stand will be frozen into a set-up position, or you will be unable to screw a bolt in far enough to set the stand upright.

Short-Term Repair: If your hardware is frozen in the correct position, simply transport the stand in a set-up position, and do not attempt to force the screw. On the other hand, if you are having difficulty getting a wingbolt to hold your stand upright, grab a roll of duct tape and tape the stand together until you can have it fixed properly. It won't look very pretty, but it will get you through a gig.

Long-Term Repair: If the screw is jammed inside the stand, it probably needs to be broken-up and removed. Then a new threaded receptor hole needs to be bored into the stand and a new screw installed. If you can take the screw out, first try to replace it with a new one, and see if it will securely hold the stand. If that doesn't work take the stand to your local drum shop and have it repaired by an expert.

Snare Hardware

Worn Out Snare Strands. If you've cranked your snare tensioning knob to its limit and still can't get a sufficient buzz from it, you've got some potentially serious problems. Obviously, you should set-up your spare snare drum if you've got one, and keep playing.

Short-Term Repair: If you don't have a spare snare, check the snare tape or cord that connects the snare strands to the throw-off and butt-plate on either side of your snare drum shell. If one of these is broken, you have two choices: play the snare without the buzz or stop and replace the cord or tape. If you don't have any spare cord or tape, you can usually cut a strip from a spare drum head, or use wire, string or any type of cord to reconnect the snare strands to the throw-off and butt plate.

However, if the cord or tape seems to be intact, the problem is probably in your throw-off, since it is the piece of snare hardware that usually has the most moving parts. If the snare tension-adjustment knob doesn't seem to sufficiently tighten the snare strands, apply additional tension by placing a drum stick in-between the hoop and the bottom of the snare throw off and/or butt plate, underneath the snare tape or cord. If that doesn't work, you can actually tape the snares to the bottom head as a last result. It will sound terrible, but at least you can keep playing. Then you should change the snares on your drum as soon as you can.

Long-Term Repair: If you still have difficulty making the snares buzz after you've changed the strands, you have a much bigger problem on your hands — most probably your bottom bearing edge (the beveled edge of the shell that contacts the head) has somehow been damaged. Don't try to correct this yourself. Take the drum to your local drum shop and have them at least check, and hopefully fix the edge for you.

ABS. A durable plastic/nylon material used in and on many percussion stands.

Adjustable angle clamp. A rack clamp that connects two horizontal support bars without the use of a leg.

Anodized steel. Electric paint process for metal in colored and brushed finishes.

ATS (Advanced Tripod System). Leg brace which utilizes separately adjustable collars to position legs.

Ball-and-socket (or 360° adjustment). A tilting mechanism used on various mounts which utlizes an ABS ball to swivel mount.

Bass drum beater. A metal shaft topped by a beater ball, which is inserted into a hole in the beater hub of a bass drum pedal.

Bass pedal spring. The spring that connects to the cam assembly and a receptor in the base of the frame of a bass drum pedal, which pulls the pedal back from the head when the pedal board isn't depressed.

Batter head. The top head of a drum which is struck.

Bearing edge. Point of drum shell where the head makes contact.

Beater hub. The bass pedal assmembly that attaches the bass drum beater to the drive shaft.

Beater pad. The pad that affixes to the bass drumhead at the point of impact.

Boom stand. A stand that has a boom arm attachment.

Brushed finish. Metal which has a slightly rough finish. Sometimes anodized, sometimes tumbled to smooth rough finishes.

Butt end (see snare butt). Usually found on the side of a snare drum opposite the throw-off. This piece holds the snares in a fixed position.

Cable hi-hat pedal. A pedal that allows the hi-hat cymbals to be positioned anywhere on a drum kit.

Cam drive. A non-tooth or toothless chain drive mechanism.

Chain drive. A pedal with a bicycle chain that connects the beater hub to the footboard.

Chrome finish. A three-step process of electrically adhering several metals to steel to give a brilliant covering.

Claw hooks. The hooks that grip the outer edge of the bass drum hoop.

Clutch. The clamping mechanism that holds the top hi-hat cymbal to the pull rod.

Counterhoop. A circular piece of steel, brass or wood that applies tension on the drumhead when the tension rods are tightened.

Counterweight. On bass drum beaters: attaches to the beater shaft to fine-tune the pedal action. On boom cymbal stands: attaches to the bottom of a boom arm to counteract the weight of the cymbal.

Cymbal sleeve. A plastic or nylon sleeve that prevents a cymbal from touching the metal rod of a cymbal stand.

cymbal stacker. Allows two cymbals to be mounted above and below each other on one stand.

Die-cast. Made by casting metal in a mold.

Double-bass pedal. A two-pedal system that enables the drummer to play a single bass drum with both feet.

Double-braced. Tripod legs constructed of two parallel pieces of stamped metal that meet and attach at both the rubber foot and the top collar.

Drop clutch. A hi-hat clutch that allows a drummer to close the hi-hat cymbals by hitting the clutch's release arm with a stick.

Elliptical leg base. A stand leg base which utilizes round or oval tube stock.

Rock or Turbo plate. A metal plate connected to the underside of a bass pedal's heel plate and to the bottom of the pedal's frame, replacing the standard radius rod.

Forty-Five Degree (45°) Angle System. A leg system that supports the weight of an item on an angle.

Free-floating. Drum tensioning hardware which does not touch the shell.

Hardened steel. Steel which has gone through a special process of heating and cooling to increase its strength.

Hide-away boom. A cymbal stand which can double as a straight or boom stand.

Hi-hat stabilizer. Secures cable hi-hat pedals to other pieces of hardware.

Knurl. A small projecting ridge to assist in gripping an object.

L-rod. L-shaped rod used to mount percussion instruments.

Lug. The bracket attached to a drum that accepts a tension rod.

Lug nut. The recpetacle which fits inside a lug and accepts a tension rod, allowing a drum to be tuned.

Memory clamp. Holds chosen positions on stands and rack systems.

Multi-clamp. A clamp which mounts various instruments and/or stands to each other. (Traditionally used on cymbal stands.)

Nodal lug mounting. A method of mounting a drum's lugs at points on the shell where the vibrations from stick hits converge.

Nylon bushing. Internal collar that prevents metal-to-metal contact within a stand.

Pedal board. The flat surface of a bass or hi-hat pedal which is activated by foot pressure, usually consisting of a foot plate and a heel plate, connected by a hinge.

Percussion table. Flat table usually padded with edges to hold hand percussion instruments.

Platform stand. A stand used to mount several items.

Pot metal. Slang for casted zinc.

Powder coating. Special color process which bakes paint onto metal.

Pull rod. The internal drive of a hi-hat pedal.

Rachet. A wheel or bar bearing a series of notches in which a pivoted tongue engages to prevent backward movement.

Rack multi-clamp. A clamp which mounts instruments to a rack system.

Rack system. A combination of horizontal and vertical bars and clamps on which instruments are mounted.

Resonant head. Bottom head used on tom toms and snare drums or the front of a bass drum.

Single-braced hardware. Tripod legs made of a solitary piece of stamped metal tipped with a rubber foot.

Snare basket. The upper assembly of a snare stand which cradles the snare drum.

Snare butt. The clamping device that holds the snare strands firmly on the side of the shell opposite the throw-off.

Snare cord (or straps). Holds snares to throw-off and butt assembly.

Snares. Coiled metal strands which vibrate against the bottom (snare side) head of a snare drum.

Snare side head. The thinner head found on the bottom of a snare drum.

Spanner system. A horizontal rack bar that connects to two cymbal or tom stands.

Sproket drive. A chain-drive mechanism with teeth.

Stand. A telescoping series of tubular tiers held vertically by a tripod base that suspends an instrument.

Straight stand. A stand that has a single central shaft that is vertical to the floor.

Strap drive. A pedal with a leather or synthetic strap that connects the beater hub to the footboard.

Swivel cam. A protruding, circular part at the top of a bass pedal's frame which transmits a back-and-forth motion to the horizontal shaft supporting the beater hub.

T-clamp. The clamp that connects a leg to a rack's support bar.

Tension rod (or key rod). Flat-nosed straight-sided screws that insert into a drum's lugs and apply pressure to the counterhoop.

Throw-off. A locking mechanism that provides tension on the snare strands.

Tier. The modular tubes that nest inside one another in the central body of a stand.

T-leg system. A leg system found on rack systems which has equal balance in the front and rear.

Tripod. A three-legged base.

Tom mount. The bracket which accepts a tom tom arm to mount a tom-tom to a bass drum, rack or stand.

Tube lug. A tubular, low-mass lug, commonly made of brass.

U joint. Metal assembly which allows movement with multiple position adjustment. Usually connects secondary pedal to primary pedal on double-pedal systems.

Washer. A metal or felt disc that sits between two objects.

Wingscrew. A screw with wing-like finger grips.

HARDWARE
GLOSSARY

ABOUT THE AUTHOR

Andy Doerschuk is the Editor of DRUM! magazine, a free publication for drummers that is available on the West Coast. He is also a contributor to *Musician*, *Rhythm* (U.K.) and *Fachblatt* (Germany) magazines, the author of *the Bass Book* and the former Editor of *Drums & Drumming* and *Bass Player* magazines. He has also experienced a full career as a drummer, having performed live and/or recording with Chet Atkins, John Kay & Steppenwolf, Rick Derringer, Billy Vera & The Beaters, Pat Travers, the Naughty Sweeties, Henry Kaiser and Leslie West.

ABOUT GIBRALTAR HARDWARE

Gibraltar Hardware is a division of Kaman Music Corporation, which also includes Toca Percussion and Legend drums. Gibraltar Hardware manufacturers a full-line of drum and percussion hardware for beginners through advanced players is available throughout the world. Gibraltar Hardware is endorsed by such great artists as Russ McKinnon, Joe Porcaro, Luis Conte, Bobby Rondinelli, Kevin Ricard, Steve Reid, Tris Imboden, Van Romaine, Jonathan Moffett, Steve Forman, Michael Baker and Bashiri Johnson.